Quiche Cookbook

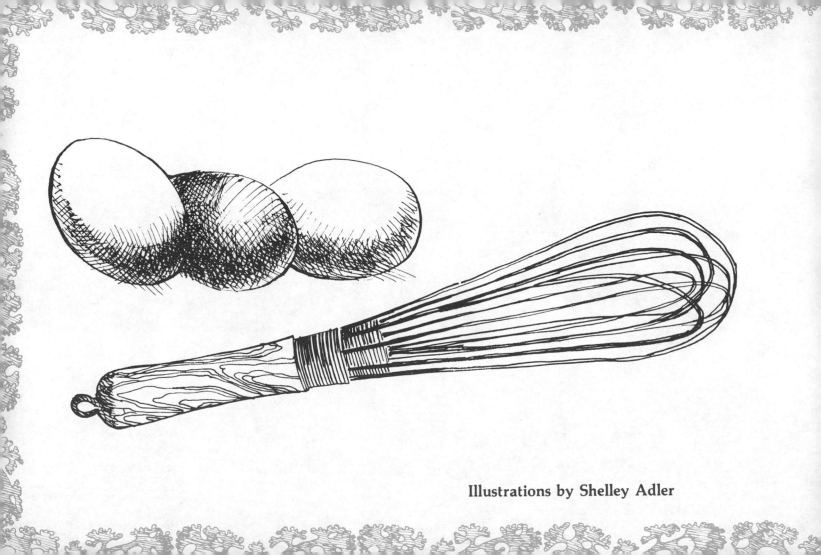

Illustrations by Shelley Adler

Quiche Cookbook

EDIE AND TOM HILTON

a **Ward Ritchie Press** book
distributed by Crown Publishers, Inc.
New York

Library of Congress Catalog Card Number: 76-16268
ISBN: 0-517-53766-4

PRINTED IN THE UNITED STATES OF AMERICA

13   12   11   10

ABOUT THE AUTHORS

Edie Hilton runs a very successful exclusive catering service in Beverly Hills, California, where she has been preparing and serving quiches for some of the most discerning appetites in the world.

Tom Hilton, her husband, is a writer.

CONTENTS

WHAT IS A QUICHE? 8
THE RIGHT EQUIPMENT 10
THE PASTRY SHELL 12
TECHNIQUES FOR SUCCESS 17
TABLE OF QUICHES

CHEESE
Swiss 20
Cottage 22
Mozzarella 24
Roquefort 26
Grape 28
Cherry 30
Brie 32
Bazaar 34

VEGETABLE
Onion 38
Onion and Cheddar 40
Onion and Swiss 42
Onion and Tomato 44
Leek 46
Tomato 48

Tomato and Cheddar 50
Tomato/Cheese/Onion Ring 52
Tomato and Vegetable 54
Eggplant 56
Ratatouille 58
Moussaka 60
Vegetarian Eggplant 62
Zucchini 64
Zucchini and Bacon 66
Zucchini and Green Chile 68
Asparagus 70
Broccoli and Cheese 72
Spicy Cauliflower 74
Corn 76
Mushroom 78
Mushroom and Bacon 80
Savory Potato 82
Spinach Noodle/Mushroom 84
Vermicelli 86
Spinach 88
Spinach and Cheese 90
Spinach and Anchovy 92
Chile 94
Christmas 96
St. Tropez 98

MEAT

Lorraine Henri	102
Alsace Lorraine	104
Bacon and Mushroom	106
Bacon and Veal	108
Ham	110
Ham and Cheese	112
Ham and Potato	114
Maison Edie	116
Sausage and Leek	118
Italian Sausage and Cheese	120
Cheddar Links	122
Meat and Cheese	124
Beef and Onion	126
Curried	128
Lamb and Artichoke	130
Chicken and Almond	132
Chicken and Broccoli	134
Chicken and Water Chestnut	136
Chicken Liver	138

SEAFOOD

Anchovy and Tomato	142
Anchovy and Greek Olive	144
Tuna au Gratin	146
Tuna and Olive	148
Tuna and Sardine	150
Salmon Souffle	152
Smoked Salmon	156
Salmon and Endive	154
Shrimp	158
Danish Shrimp	160
Shrimp and Egg	162
Shrimp and Broccoli	164
Rockefeller	166
Angels on Horseback	168
Scallops	170
Mussels	172
Crab	174
Crab and Avocado	176
King Crab	178
Lobster	180
Lobster Royale	182
Edie's Quiche Friday	184
Mixed Seafood	186

WHAT IS A QUICHE?

Classically, a quiche is a custard tart filled with bacon, cheese, or a combination of the two. It is a favorite of long-standing in the catalog of country French cooking. But today the definition has been extended to any pie shell flavored with any variety and combination of cheeses, vegetables, meat, or seafood. Quiches are a fascinating change from routine menu fare. They are extremely economical to prepare in terms of both time and money. Variations seem limited only by the cook's imagination and the seasonal or regional availability of potential ingredients.

In addition, quiches are indeed multipurpose menu items. What other food can you name that is as equally suitable for hors d'oeuvres and appetizers, potato substitutes, and secondary main dishes as for entrees at luncheons or light suppers? The recipes in this book will serve 2 to 4 happy people as an entree or 4 to 6 delighted folks as an adjunct to a larger meal.

The recipes have been standardized to fill a 4 cup capacity container. This would include a 10 inch aluminum tart shell (with a removable bottom), a 9 inch fluted edge china quiche pan, a 9 inch pie plate, a 9 inch deep dish frozen pie shell, and a 8-1/2 removable rim pan. If what you have to use is larger, the quiche will be thinner, if smaller, you will not need as much custard mixture. Some experimentation may be necessary before you achieve a casualness about filling your pan. Keep in mind that the object is variety. Remember how many famous French specialties (onion soup, crepes suzette) were supposed to have been created by someone's having reached into the pantry and manipulated the ingredients on hand to spectacular advantage.

BON APPETIT!

Tom and Edie Hilton

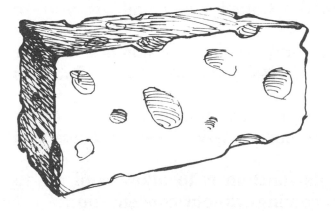

THE RIGHT EQUIPMENT

Unlike other areas of gourmet cooking, there is little specialized equipment required to prepare and serve even the most impressive of quiches. Most of what is needed would be found in the average well-equipped kitchen. The few items that you might want to acquire are both relatively inexpensive and easy to locate.

A *mouli grater* with attachments is essential for the effortless grating, coarse grating, and shredding of almost anything, especially cheese. Once you have experienced the ease with which this hand-operated gadget allows you to work, you will be hooked.

A good quality *wire whisk* is a must, not only for making quiches, but for almost any blending and beating job. It is a necessity for any recipe that calls for eggs to be beaten.

The *pastry blender* is a controversial kitchen utensil that some swear by to cut in butter particles into flour and others consciously forego and use two knives.

The *wire cooling rack* is a vital item. Its function is to allow cool air to circulate beneath the quiche shell for even cooling without condensation.

An extremely popular item in Europe now available here is the *quiche pan.* Its only advantage is that it produces a highly decorative shell with deeply fluted edges that will testify to your savoir faire. The quiche pan is available in china, which is brought to the table and served from, or aluminum with a removable rim where the free-standing quiche is transferred to a serving plate.

Chilled dough is one of the most important secrets of perfect pastry making. The best *pastry board* to achieve this is a flat piece of marble, large enough to enable you to roll out a 14 inch circle of dough, but still able to fit in the refrigerator. A piece of marble 18 by 20 inches and 1/2 inch thick would be ideal and can be obtained from a local marble supply house. If the store stocks marble rods, a length 16 to 18 inches and 2 inches in diameter makes the finest *rolling pin.*

Another piece of equipment not actually required for preparing quiches but extremely useful is a device to make hermetically sealed cooking pouches in which to store leftovers. As most quiches recipes call for a very small amount of main ingredients, the thrifty cook can package delicious odds and ends and gradually build up a "quiche bank" in the freezer.

THE PERFECT PASTRY SHELL

1-1/2 cups flour
1/4 cup butter
1/4 cup solid vegetable shortening
1/4 teaspoon salt
1/4 cup cold liquid; water or orange
   or lemon juice mixed with water

   With a mixer, blend the flour, butter, shortening, and salt until the mixture is the texture of coarse meal, or cut in the butter and shortening with a pastry blender. Add the liquid and mix with a wooden spoon and your hands until the dough comes out clean from the bowl and forms a ball. Flatten into an 8 inch round circle, wrap in wax paper, and refrigerate for 30 minutes. Place the dough on a well-floured board—formica or marble is preferred. Roll the dough into a 12 inch circle. Starting at the edge of the circle, roll the dough over the rolling pin. Gently unroll the dough onto the pan. Without forcing or stretching the dough, press it into the pan. Be careful that the dough is not too thick where the bottom and sides meet. Allow 1 inch of dough to hang over the edge of the pan. Trim off the excess. Turn the 1 inch of overhang under to form a narrow rolled rim, if you are using a pie plate. You can also either flute the edge, or make a rope edge by pinching the dough in opposite directions. To partially prebake (in order to strengthen the shell for the filling), preheat the oven to 400 degrees. With a fork, prick the sides and bottom of the shell. Set a piece of wax paper on the dough, cover it with rice or lima beans, and bake for 10 minutes. Remove the paper and the rice or beans and cool the shell. The pastry shell may be prepared 1 or 2 days ahead and refrigerated, wrapped. It may also be prepared and frozen before prebaking, then defrosted for 10 minutes at room temperature before use. Following are recipes for 2 other pastry shells made from scratch and alternatives to making your own pastry.

CREAM CHEESE PASTRY SHELL

6 ounces cream cheese
1/4 cup sweet butter
2 tablespoons heavy cream
1-1/4 cups sifted flour
1/4 teaspoon salt

Using an electric mixer, beat the cream cheese and butter together until smooth and creamy. Add the heavy cream and continue to beat for a minute or two. With a wooden spoon, slowly add the flour and mix until thoroughly combined. Roll the dough into a ball and wrap securely in wax paper. Place in the refrigerator to chill at least overnight, or better yet for several days before rolling out. Be sure to roll out between two pieces of wax paper. Once rolled out this dough is extremely fragile. The best way to transfer it to the pan is by gently rolling it around the rolling pin and unrolling it over the pan and removing the paper as you carefully slide the dough into the pan. Arrange and prebake.

PARMESAN OR CHEDDAR CHEESE PASTRY SHELL

1-1/4 cups sifted flour
1/2 cup grated Parmesan or Cheddar
   cheese
4 tablespoons butter, cut into pieces
1/4 teaspoon salt
4 to 5 tablespoons cold water

Place the flour, cheese, and salt in a mixing bowl. Cut the butter into the mixture until it reaches the consistency of coarse meal. Add the cold water a tablespoon at a time and stir with a fork while gathering the dough into a ball with the finger tips of the other hand. Add any additional water that is needed a drop at a time. Once the ball is smooth but not sticky, wrap it securely in wax paper and place in the refrigerator to chill for at least one hour before rolling out. Arrange and prebake.

BEATING THE QUICHE SHELL GAME

Many gourmet bakeries sell partially prebaked pastry shells ready to fill and pop in the oven. Make a point of locating a source in your area. Buy a few at a time and keep them in the freezer for spontaneous quiche-making occasions. You can keep on hand several boxes of pie crust sticks. Shells from this method can be prepared in minutes by simply mixing the contents of the package with water and rolling out the pastry. A quiche pan can be lined with a package of regrigerator crescent rolls. The dough is unrolled onto a floured board overlapping the perforations and rolled into a single piece about half the thickness of the original. Other types of biscuits are also appropriate. The thing to remember is not to overwork the ready-to-use dough.

The ultimate dough dodge is to use oven ready pie shells in foil pans. You must be careful to buy only the deep dish kind or you will find the crust not sturdy enough to hold up under the weight of the fillings. Choose whatever method you think will suit your taste and convenience. The selection of the best shell for any particular filling is also basically a matter of personal preference.

TECHNIQUES FOR SUCCESS

- It is essential to preheat the oven before you begin assembling the quiche.
- Carefully cover the entire surface of the quiche pan with a spray coating.
- A good quality cookie sheet must be used. One that warps in the oven after the quiche has started to bake will cause the pan to tilt and the filling to rise in a lopsided manner, if not spill over into the oven.
- The inside of the pastry shell needs to be waterproofed before filling. Paint with a lightly beaten egg white and let dry.
- Piecrust stick pastry and frozen ready to use shells do not require prebaking.
- Vegetables and meat for the fillings can be cooked the day before and stored in the refrigerator in separate airtight containers.
- Cheese can be grated a few hours before use and stored covered in the refrigerator.
- To unmold a tin quiche pan, center the removable bottom over a coffee can and slide down the tart ring. After the quiche has cooled for 5 to 10 minutes on a wire rack, slip a spatula underneath the quiche and move it all around and carefully slide the quiche itself onto a serving plate.
- Baked quiches can be kept in the refrigerator for several days and reheated, or some prefer to eat them cold (at room temperature).
- It is not recommended that quiches be frozen.

Cheese Quiches

SWISS CHEESE QUICHE

1 pastry shell
3 eggs
2 egg yolks
2 cups milk, scalded
1/2 teaspoon salt
1/8 teaspoon black pepper
1/8 teaspoon nutmeg
6 ounces Swiss cheese, grated

GARNISH
1 chile pepper, thinly sliced
1 pitted ripe olive, thinly sliced
1 stuffed green olive, thinly sliced
Several parsley sprigs, plus
   1 tablespoon chopped parsley
Sprinkling of paprika

Lightly beat the eggs and yolks with a wire whisk. Add the milk and seasonings and blend until smooth. Slowly stir in the grated Swiss cheese. Set the pastry shell on a cookie sheet and carefully pour in the cheese-custard mixture. Preheat the oven to 375°. Bake on the center shelf of the oven for 25 to 30 minutes, or until the top is puffed up and a knife inserted in the center of the custard comes out clean. Remove from the oven and carefully slide onto a wire rack for 5 to 10 minutes to let the custard set. Garnish and serve hot.

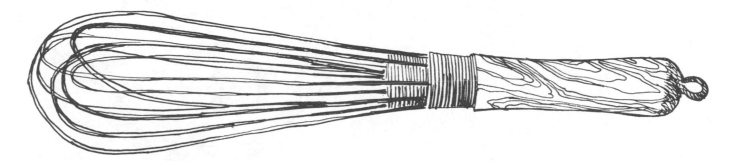

COTTAGE CHEESE QUICHE

1 pastry shell
1-1/2 cups cottage cheese with chives
4 eggs
3/4 cup half-and-half
1/2 teaspoon salt
1/8 teaspoon white pepper
1/4 pound Swiss cheese, grated
3/4 cup canned French fried onion rings

Combine the cottage cheese, eggs, half-and-half and seasonings and blend until smooth. Spread half the grated Swiss cheese over the bottom of the pastry shell. Set the shell on a cookie sheet and carefully pour in the cheese-custard mixture. Sprinkle with the rest of the cheese. Preheat oven to 350°. Bake on the center shelf of the oven for 30 to 35 minutes. Remove from the oven and place onion rings on the top of the quiche. Return to the oven and bake 10 minutes more, or until a knife inserted in the center of the custard comes out clean. Remove from the oven and carefully slide onto a wire rack for 5 to 10 minutes to let the custard set. Garnish, if desired, and serve hot.

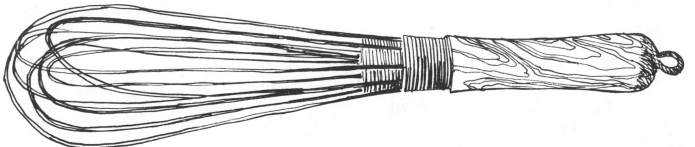

MOZZARELLA CHEESE QUICHE

1 pastry shell
1/4 pound mozzarella cheese, diced
1/3 cup grated Parmesan cheese
3 tablespoons finely chopped parsley
1/4 teaspoon salt
1/8 teaspoon black pepper
4 eggs
1-1/2 cups half-and-half
1/4 teaspoon salt
1/8 teaspoon black pepper
1/8 teaspoon nutmeg

GARNISH
1 teaspoon chopped chives
1 pitted ripe olive, thinly sliced
1 stuffed green olive, thinly sliced
Sprinkling of paprika

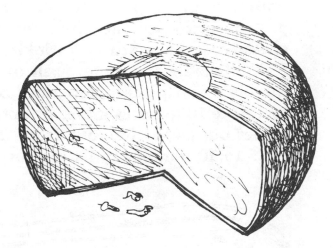

Mix together the cheeses, parsley, salt and pepper and set aside. Lightly beat the eggs with a wire whisk. Add the half-and-half and seasonings and blend until smooth. Slowly add the cheese mixture to the custard, stirring constantly. Set the pastry shell on a cookie sheet and carefully pour in the cheese-custard mixture. Preheat oven to 375°. Bake on the center shelf of the oven for 35 minutes, or until the top is puffed up and browned and a knife inserted in the center of the custard comes out clean. Remove from the oven and carefully slide onto a wire rack for 5 to 10 minutes to let the custard set. Garnish and serve hot.

ROQUEFORT CHEESE QUICHE

1 pastry shell
3 ounces Roquefort cheese
6 ounces cream cheese
2 tablespoons butter, softened
3 tablespoons heavy cream
3 eggs
1 cup half-and-half
1/2 tablespoon chopped chives
1/4 teaspoon salt
1/3 teaspoon white pepper
1/8 teaspoon cayenne pepper

GARNISH
Several parsley sprigs, plus
   1 tablespoon chopped parsley
1 pitted ripe olive, thinly sliced
1 stuffed green olive, thinly sliced
Sprinkling of paprika

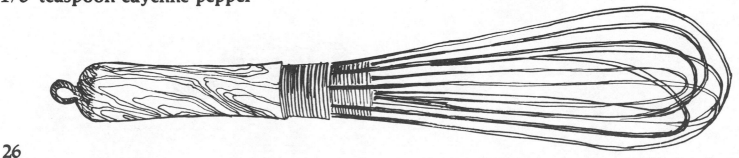

Combine the cheeses, butter, and cream with a fork. Lightly beat in the eggs and half-and-half. The mixture will be lumpy and should be forced through a sieve. Stir in the chives and seasonings. Set the pastry shell on a cookie sheet and carefully pour in the cheese-custard mixture. Preheat oven to 375°. Bake on the center shelf of the oven for 25 minutes, or until the top is puffed up and browned and a knife inserted in the center of the custard comes out clean. Remove from the oven and carefully slide onto a wire rack for 5 to 10 minutes to let the custard set. Garnish and serve hot.

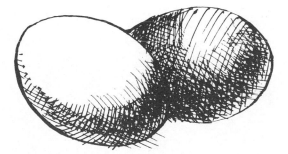

GRAPE CHEESE QUICHE

1 pastry shell
1/2 pound Grape cheese, chilled
3 eggs
2 egg yolks
1-1/2 cups half-and-half
1/2 teaspoon dry mustard
1/4 teaspoon nutmeg
1/4 teaspoon salt
1/8 teaspoon cayenne pepper

Cut the cheese into small pieces and spread over the bottom of the pastry shell. Lightly beat the eggs and yolks with a wire whisk. Add the half-and-half and seasonings and blend until smooth. Set the pastry shell on a cookie sheet and carefully pour in cheese-custard mixture. Preheat oven to 375°. Bake on the center shelf of the oven for 35 minutes, or until the top is puffed up and browned and a knife inserted into the center of the custard comes out clean. Remove from the oven and carefully slide onto a wire rack for 5 to 10 minutes to let the custard set. Serve hot.

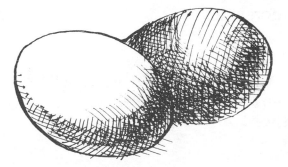

CHERRY CHEESE QUICHE

1 pastry shell
1/2 pound Cherry cheese, chilled
3 eggs
2 egg yolks
1 cup heavy cream, scalded
1/2 cup sour cream
1 teaspoon Dijon mustard
1/4 teaspoon nutmeg
1/4 teaspoon sugar
1/4 teaspoon salt

GARNISH
4 red maraschino cherries, thinly sliced
4 green maraschino cherries,
    thinly sliced

Cut the cheese into small pieces and spread over the bottom of the pastry shell. Lightly beat the eggs and egg yolks with a wire whisk. Add the heavy cream, sour cream, and seasonings and blend until smooth. Set the pastry shell on a cookie sheet and carefully pour in the cheese-custard mixture. Preheat oven to 350°. Bake on the center shelf of the oven for 30 minutes, or until the top is puffed up and browned and a knife inserted in the center of the custard comes out clean. Remove from the oven and carefully slide onto a wire rack for 5 to 10 minutes to let the custard set. Garnish and serve hot.

BRIE CHEESE QUICHE

1 pastry shell
3 ounces Brie cheese (without crust)
6 ounces small curd cottage cheese
2 tablespoons butter, softened
2 tablespoons heavy cream
3 eggs
1 cup half-and-half
1/2 tablespoon chopped chives
1/4 teaspoon salt
1/8 teaspoon white pepper
1/8 teaspoon cayenne pepper

GARNISH
Several parsley sprigs, plus
    1 tablespoon chopped parsley
1 pitted ripe olive, thinly sliced
1 stuffed green olive, thinly sliced
Sprinkling of paprika and/or nutmeg

Blend together the cheeses, butter, and cream. Lightly beat in the eggs and half-and-half. The mixture will be lumpy and should be forced through a sieve. Add the chives and seasonings. Set the pastry shell on a cookie sheet and carefully pour in the cheese-custard mixture. Preheat oven to 375°. Bake on the center shelf of the oven for 25 minutes, or until top is puffed up and browned and a knife inserted in the center of the custard comes out clean. Remove from the oven and carefully slide onto a wire rack for 5 to 10 minutes to let the custard set.

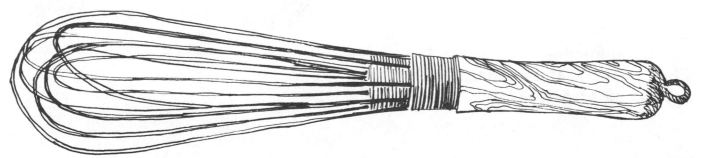

CHEESE BAZAAR QUICHE

1 pastry shell
2 eggs
2 egg yolks
1-1/2 cups heavy cream
3 tablespoons finely chopped parsley
1/4 teaspoon salt
1/4 teaspoon black pepper
1/8 teaspoon nutmeg
1/2 pound assorted cheeses, grated
1/4 cup grated Parmesan cheese

GARNISH
Canned pimentos, thinly sliced
Chile peppers, thinly sliced
Sprinkling of paprika

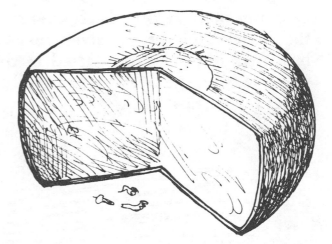

34

Lightly beat the eggs and egg yolks with a wire whisk. Add the cream, parsley, and seasonings and blend until smooth. Adding a little at a time, blend in the cheeses. Set the pastry shell on a cookie sheet and carefully pour in the cheese-custard mixture. Sprinkle with the grated Parmesan cheese. Preheat oven to 375°. Bake on center shelf of the oven for 30 to 40 minutes, or until the top is puffed up and browned and a knife inserted in the center of the custard comes out clean. Remove from the oven and carefully slide onto a wire rack for 5 to 10 minutes to let the custard set. Garnish and serve hot.

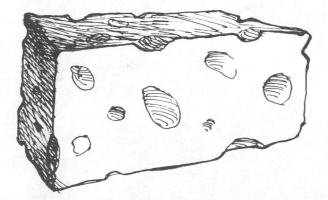

Vegetable Quiches

ONION QUICHE

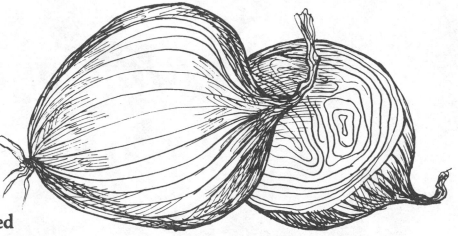

1 pastry shell
3 tablespoons butter
1 tablespoon vegetable oil
2 pounds onions, minced
1-1/2 tablespoons flour
2 eggs
2/3 cup heavy cream
1 teaspoon salt
1/8 teaspoon black pepper
1/8 teaspoon nutmeg
2 ounces Swiss cheese, grated

GARNISH
2 pitted ripe olives, thinly sliced
2 strips pimento, finely chopped

Melt the butter in a heavy skillet, add the oil and onions, and cook over a very low heat for 5 to 10 minutes, or until the onions are tender and golden. Sprinkle the onions with flour, mix well, and cook for several minutes more and then set aside. Lightly beat the eggs with a wire whisk and add the cream and seasonings and blend until smooth. Mix in the onions and grated cheese. Set the pastry shell on a cookie sheet and carefully pour in the custard-onion mixture. Preheat oven to 375°. Bake on the center shelf of the oven for 30 minutes, or until the top is puffed up and browned and a knife inserted in the center of the custard comes out clean. Remove from the oven and carefully slide onto a wire rack for 5 to 10 minutes to let the custard set. Garnish and serve hot.

ONION AND CHEDDAR QUICHE

1 pastry shell
3 tablespoons butter
3 large onions, thinly sliced
4 eggs
1-1/2 cups half-and-half
1/4 pound sharp Cheddar cheese, grated
1 teaspoon parsley flakes
1-1/2 teaspoons celery salt
1/8 teaspoon white pepper

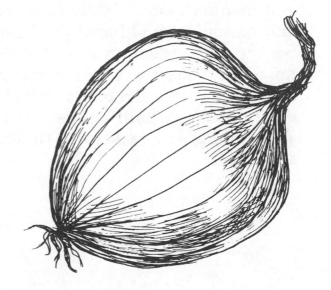

Melt the butter in a heavy skillet, add the onions, and cook for 5 to 10 minutes until they are tender and golden. Lightly beat the eggs with a wire whisk. Add the eggs, half-and-half, cheese, and seasonings to the onions and stir until smooth. Set the pastry shell on a cookie sheet and carefully pour in the onion-custard mixture. Preheat oven to 325°. Bake on the center shelf of the oven for 30 to 40 minutes, or until the top is puffed up and browned and a knife inserted in the center of the custard comes out clean. Remove from the oven and carefully slide onto a wire rack for 5 to 10 minutes to let the custard set. Garnish, if desired, and serve hot.

ONION AND SWISS CHEESE QUICHE

1 pastry shell
3 tablespoons butter
1/2 pound onions, thinly sliced
1/4 teaspoon salt
1/8 teaspoon black pepper
2 ounces Swiss cheese, grated
4 eggs
1-1/2 cups heavy cream
1/4 cup dry white wine
1/4 teaspoon salt
1/8 teaspoon black pepper
1/8 teaspoon nutmeg

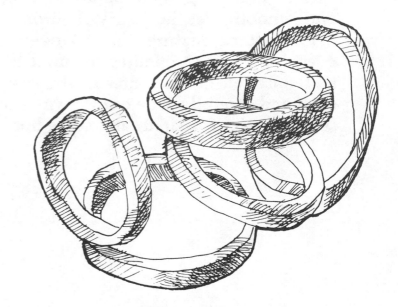

Melt the butter in a heavy skillet, add the onions, and cook for 5 to 10 minutes, or until tender and golden. Stir in the salt and pepper. Spoon the mixture into the pastry shell and sprinkle with the grated cheese. Lightly beat the eggs with a wire whisk. Add the cream, wine, and seasonings and blend until smooth. Set the pastry shell on a cookie sheet and carefully pour in the custard mixture. Preheat oven to 375°. Bake on the center shelf of the oven for 40 minutes, or until the top is puffed up and browned and a knife inserted in the center of the custard comes out clean. Remove from the oven and carefully slide onto a wire rack for 5 to 10 minutes to let the custard set. Garnish, if desired, and serve hot.

ONION AND TOMATO QUICHE

1 pastry shell
4 tablespoons butter
2 Bermuda onions, sliced thick
3 eggs
2 egg yolks
1-1/2 cups milk, scalded
3 ounces Swiss cheese, grated
1 teaspoon Dijon mustard
1 teaspoon dry mustard
1 teaspoon salt
1/2 teaspoon nutmeg
1/4 teaspoon cayenne pepper
2 large tomatoes, sliced thickly
1/3 cup seasoned bread crumbs
1/3 cup grated Parmesan cheese
1 package frozen onion rings

GARNISH
Several parsley sprigs, plus
   1 tablespoon chopped parsley
1 pimento, thinly sliced
1 chile pepper, thinly sliced
1 pitted ripe olive, thinly sliced
1 stuffed green olive, thinly sliced
6 thin tomato wedges
Sprinkling of paprika

Melt the butter in a heavy skillet, add the onions, and cook for 5 to 10 minutes, or until tender and golden. Set aside. Lightly beat the eggs and yolks with a wire whisk. Add the milk, cheese, and seasonings and blend until smooth. Stir in the onions. Sprinkle half the crumbs in the pastry shell. Coat the tomato slices with the remaining crumbs and spread over the bottom of the shell. Sprinkle with the grated Parmesan cheese. Set the pastry shell on a cookie sheet and carefully pour in the onion-custard mixture. Prepare the frozen onion rings according to package directions and set aside. Preheat oven to 350°. Bake on the center shelf of the oven for 30 to 40 minutes, or until the top is puffed up and browned and a knife inserted in the center of the custard comes out clean. Remove from the oven, arrange the onion rings on top, and return to the oven for 5 minutes, or until the onion rings are heated through. Remove from the oven, garnish, and serve hot.

LEEK QUICHE

1 pastry shell
4 tablespoons butter
1/2 cup water
1 teaspoon salt
3 cups leeks (white parts only), sliced
3 eggs
1-1/2 cups heavy cream
1/4 teaspoon nutmeg
1/8 teaspoon black pepper
2 ounces Swiss cheese, grated
2 wedges processed Gruyere cheese

In a heavy skillet, melt the butter, add the water, salt, and leeks, and stir well. Cover and cook over a medium heat for 10 to 12 minutes, or until the pan juices have almost completely evaporated. Lower the heat and cook the leeks until they are soft. Drain and set aside. Lightly beat the eggs with a wire whisk. Add the cream and seasonings and blend until smooth. Stir in the leeks and half the grated Swiss cheese. Set the pastry shell on a cookie sheet and carefully pour in the cheese-custard mixture. Sprinkle with the remaining Swiss cheese. Cut each wedge of Gruyere cheese into 4 slices and arrange in a pinwheel pattern on the top of the quiche. Preheat oven to 375°. Bake on the center shelf of the oven for 30 minutes, or until the top is puffed up and browned and a knife inserted in the center of the custard comes out clean. Remove from the oven and carefully slide onto a wire rack for 5 to 10 minutes to let the custard set. Garnish, if desired, and serve hot.

TOMATO QUICHE

1 pastry shell
1/4 cup minced onion
2 garlic cloves, minced
4 tablespoons olive oil
2 pounds firm ripe tomatoes,
    peeled, seeded, and chopped
1 teaspoon sugar
1/8 teaspoon salt
1/8 teaspoon black pepper
1 egg
3 egg yolks
8 anchovy fillets
1 tablespoon anchovy oil
3 tablespoons finely chopped parsley
2 tablespoons basil

1 teaspoon oregano
1 tablespoon tomato paste
10 pitted ripe olives, halved
1/3 cup grated Parmesan cheese
1 ounce Swiss cheese, grated

GARNISH
1 tablespoon basil or chopped parsley

In a heavy skillet, saute the onion and garlic in 2 tablespoons olive oil for 5 to 10 minutes, or until the onion is tender and golden. Slowly add the tomatoes, sugar, salt and pepper. Cook over a moderate heat until most of the moisture has evaporated and the mixture has thickened to a heavy paste. Cool. Lightly beat the egg and yolks with a wire whisk and stir into mixture. Add the anchovies plus 1 tablespoon anchovy oil, parsley, remaining olive oil, basil, tomato paste, oregano, and salt and pepper to taste. Set the pastry shell on a cookie sheet and carefully pour in the vegetable mixture. Sprinkle with olives and grated cheeses. Preheat oven to 375°. Bake on the center shelf of the oven for 25 to 30 minutes, or until the top is puffed up and browned and a knife inserted in the center of the custard comes out clean. Remove from the oven and carefully slide onto a wire rack for 5 to 10 minutes to let the custard set. Garnish and serve hot.

TOMATO AND CHEDDAR QUICHE

1 pastry shell
1 green onion, minced
1 tablespoon butter
1 can condensed cream of tomato soup
1/4 pound sharp Cheddar cheese, grated
1/2 teaspoon Dijon mustard
1/2 teaspoon basil
4 eggs
1/2 cup half-and-half
1/2 teaspoon salt
1/4 teaspoon pepper

GARNISH
1 hardboiled egg, finely chopped
1 teaspoon chopped chives
1/2 teaspoon nutmeg
1 pitted ripe olive, thinly sliced
1 stuffed green olive, thinly sliced

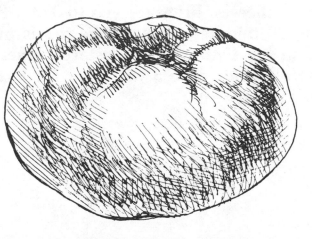

Melt the butter in a heavy skillet, add the green onion and cook for 3 to 4 minutes over a low heat. Stir in the soup, grated cheese, mustard, and basil. Simmer until the cheese has melted, and stir to blend. Cool. Lightly beat the eggs with a wire whisk. Add the half-and-half and seasonings and blend until smooth. Stir in the tomato-cheese mixture. Set the pastry shell on a cookie sheet and carefully pour in the tomato-cheese mixture. Preheat oven to 350°. Bake on the center shelf of the oven for 30 to 35 minutes, or until the top is puffed up and browned and a knife inserted in the center of the custard comes out clean. Remove from the oven and carefully slide onto a wire rack for 5 to 10 minutes to let the custard set. Garnish and serve hot.

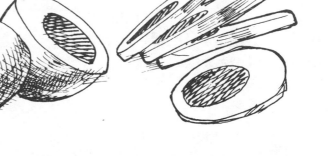

TOMATO, CHEESE, ONION RING QUICHE

1 pastry shell
1 package frozen onion rings
2 large tomatoes, thinly sliced
2 ounces Swiss cheese, grated
2 ounces mild Cheddar cheese, grated
3 eggs
1-1/2 cups half-and-half
1 teaspoon garlic salt
1/4 teaspoon black pepper
1/4 teaspoon nutmeg

GARNISH
1 tablespoon chopped parsley
1 pitted ripe olive, thinly sliced
Sprinkling of paprika

Prepare the onion rings according to package directions. Spread half the rings over the bottom of the pastry shell. Cover with half the tomato slices and sprinkle with half the grated cheeses. Repeat. Lightly beat the eggs with a wire whisk. Add the half-and-half, and seasonings and blend until smooth. Set the pastry shell on a cookie sheet and carefully pour in the custard mixture. Preheat oven to 350°. Bake on the center shelf of the oven for 30 to 40 minutes, or until the top is puffed up and browned and a knife inserted in the center of the custard comes out clean. Remove from the oven and carefully slide onto a wire rack for 5 to 10 minutes to let the custard set. Garnish and serve hot.

TOMATO AND VEGETABLE QUICHE

1 pastry shell
2 tablespoons butter
2 large onions, thinly sliced
1 garlic clove, crushed
3 medium tomatoes, peeled and chopped
1 small zucchini, thinly sliced
2 tablespoons chopped parsley
1/2 teaspoon basil
1/4 teaspoon salt
1/8 teaspoon black pepper
2 tablespoons grated Parmesan cheese
3 eggs
1/4 pound Swiss cheese, grated

GARNISH
Several parsley sprigs
2 cherry tomatoes, thinly sliced
Sprinkling of paprika

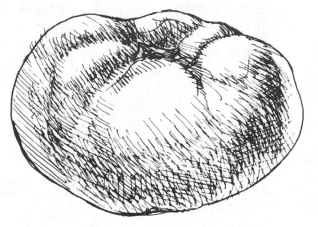

Heat the butter in a heavy skillet, add the onions and garlic, and cook for 5 to 10 minutes or until the onions are soft and golden. Stir in the tomatoes, zucchini, parsley, basil, salt and pepper. Simmer on a low heat for about 10 minutes. Sprinkle the pastry shell with the Parmesan cheese. Beat the eggs lightly with a wire whisk, cool the vegetable mixture, and blend in the eggs. Set the pastry shell on a cookie sheet and carefully pour in the vegetable-egg mixture. Sprinkle with the grated Swiss cheese. Preheat oven to 425°. Bake on the center shelf of the oven for 25 to 30 minutes, or until the top is puffed up and browned and a knife inserted in the center of the custard comes out clean. Remove from the oven and carefully slide onto a wire rack for 5 to 10 minutes to let the custard set. Garnish and serve hot.

EGGPLANT QUICHE

1 pastry shell
3 tablespoons Dijon mustard
1 ounce Swiss cheese, grated
1-1/2 pounds eggplant, peeled and diced
2/3 cup vegetable oil
1/4 pound bacon
3 eggs
1-1/2 cups canned plum tomatoes,
     pureed
2 tablespoons chopped basil
2 tablespoons chopped parsley
1/4 teaspoon salt
1/8 teaspoon pepper

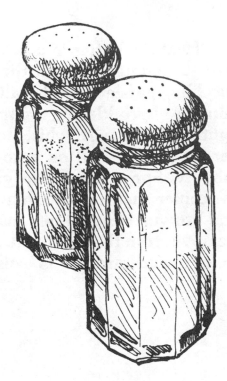

Brush the bottom and sides of the pastry shell with the mustard and sprinkle with the grated cheese. Soak the eggplant in salted water for 30 minutes. Rinse and drain on paper towels. Heat the oil in a heavy skillet and saute the eggplant over a moderate heat for about 10 minutes, or until soft and lightly browned. Drain on paper towels. Pour off any remaining oil. Cut bacon into small pieces and fry in the same pan until crisp. Remove and drain on paper towels. Lightly beat the eggs with a wire whisk. Slowly add the diced eggplant, bacon, tomatoes, herbs, and seasonings. Set the pastry shell on a cookie sheet and carefully pour in the filling mixture. Preheat oven to 375°. Bake on the center shelf of the oven 20 to 25 minutes, or until the top is puffed up and browned and a knife inserted in the center of the custard comes out clean. Remove from the oven and carefully slide onto a wire rack for 5 to 10 minutes to let the custard set. Garnish and serve hot.

RATATOUILLE QUICHE

1 pastry shell
1/3 cup olive oil
2 garlic cloves, chopped
1 onion, peeled and sliced
1-1/2 tablespoons flour
1 small eggplant, peeled and sliced
1 zucchini, scrubbed and sliced
1 green pepper, seeded and sliced
2 small tomatoes, peeled and sliced
1 tablespoon capers
3 eggs
1-1/2 cups half-and-half
1/2 teaspoon salt
1/4 teaspoon black pepper
1/2 cup grated Parmesan cheese
1/4 teaspoon nutmeg

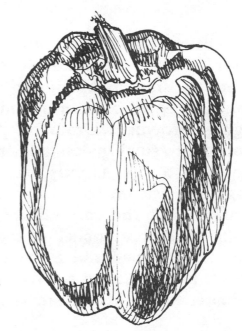

Heat the oil in a heavy skillet and saute the garlic and onion for 5 to 10 minutes, or until the onion is tender and golden. Lightly flour the remaining vegetables (except the tomatoes) and add to the skillet. Cover and cook over a low heat for about 30 minutes, stirring occasionally. Add the tomatoes and simmer uncovered until the mixture is thick. Add the capers and set aside to cool. Lightly beat the eggs with a wire whisk and add the half-and-half and seasonings and blend until smooth. Set the pastry shell on a cookie sheet and spoon in the vegetable mixture. Carefully pour in the custard. Sprinkle with the grated Parmesan cheese and nutmeg. Preheat oven to 350°. Bake on the center shelf of the oven for 35 minutes, or until the top is puffed up and browned and a knife inserted in the center of the custard comes out clean. Remove from the oven, and carefully slide onto a wire rack for 5 to 10 minutes to let the custard set. Serve hot.

MOUSSAKA QUICHE

1 pastry shell
1 eggplant, peeled and sliced
2 tablespoons flour
1/2 cup olive oil
1/2 cup finely chopped onions
1 garlic clove, finely chopped
1/2 pound lean ground beef or lamb
1/4 pound mushrooms, thinly sliced
1-1/2 ounce package dry spaghetti
   sauce mix
1 teaspoon oregano
1/4 teaspoon cinnamon
1 bay leaf, crushed
1/2 teaspoon salt
1/4 teaspoon black pepper

2 ounces sharp Cheddar cheese, grated
2 firm tomatoes, thinly sliced
3 eggs
1 cup heavy cream
1/4 cup sherry

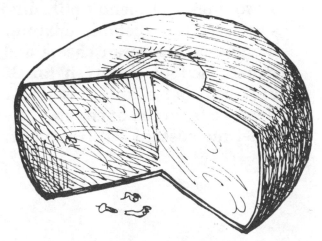

Soak the eggplant in salted water for 30 minutes, rinse, and drain. Dredge the eggplant in flour. Put half the olive oil in a heavy skillet and saute the eggplant until brown. Drain on paper towels. Add the rest of the oil to the skillet and saute the onions, garlic, meat, and mushrooms for about 10 minutes. Mix the spaghetti sauce according to package directions to make one cup, and add to meat mixture. Stir in the oregano, cinnamon, bay leaf, salt and pepper. Simmer over a low heat for about 20 minutes. Drain all liquid from the mixture. Spread half the eggplant over the bottom of the pastry shell. Cover with half the meat mixture, sprinkle with half the grated cheese, and add half the tomatoes. Repeat. Lightly beat the eggs with a wire whisk. Add the cream and sherry and blend until smooth. Set the pastry shell on a cookie sheet and carefully pour in the custard mixture. Preheat oven to 375°. Bake on the center shelf for 35 minutes, or until top is puffed up and browned and a knife inserted in the center of the custard comes out clean. Remove from the oven and carefully slide onto a wire rack for 5 to 10 minutes to let the custard set. Garnish, if desired, and serve hot.

VEGETARIAN EGGPLANT QUICHE

1 pastry shell
2 tablespoons grated Parmesan cheese
1 eggplant, peeled and diced
2 tablespoons olive oil
1 onion, finely chopped
17 ounce can plum tomatoes, drained
1/2 teaspoon salt
1/8 teaspoon pepper
1/4 teaspoon oregano
1/4 teaspoon basil
4 eggs

GARNISH
Several parsley sprigs
1 pitted ripe olive, thinly sliced

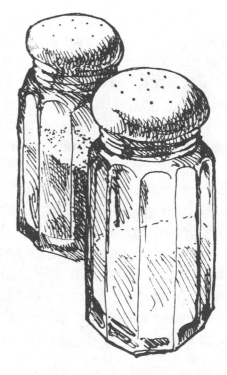

If the pastry shell is made fresh for this recipe, the grated Parmesan cheese can be mixed with the dough before rolling out. Otherwise, sprinkle into the shell. Soak the eggplant in salted water for 30 minutes. Rinse and drain. Heat the oil in a heavy skillet and saute the onions for 5 to 10 minutes or until tender and golden. Slowly add the eggplant and cook until soft but not brown. Gradually add the tomatoes and simmer for 5 minutes while mashing them. Stir in salt, pepper, oregano, and basil. Mix thoroughly and remove from heat. Lightly beat the eggs with a wire whisk and slowly stir them into the tomato mixture. Set the pastry shell on a cookie sheet and carefully pour in the filling mixture. Preheat oven to 375°. Bake on the center shelf of the oven for 25 minutes, or until the top is puffed up and browned and a knife inserted in the center of the custard comes out clean. Remove from the oven and carefully slide onto a wire rack for 5 to 10 minutes to let the custard set. Garnish and serve hot.

ZUCCHINI QUICHE

1 pastry shell
4 tablespoons butter
2 pounds zucchini, sliced
1/2 teaspoon seasoned salt
1/4 teaspoon white pepper
1/2 cup seasoned breadcrumbs
3/4 cup chopped parsley
3 eggs
1-1/2 cups half-and-half
1/8 teaspoon cayenne pepper
Dash Tabasco sauce
1/8 teaspoon nutmeg

In a heavy skillet, melt the butter and saute the zucchini with seasoned salt and pepper until tender. Spread half the zucchini over the bottom of the pastry shell. Sprinkle with half the bread crumbs and half the chopped parsley. Dust with salt and pepper. Repeat. Lightly beat the eggs with a wire whisk. Add the half-and-half and seasonings and blend until smooth. Set the pastry shell on a cookie sheet and carefully pour in the custard mixture. Sprinkle with nutmeg. Preheat oven to 375°. Bake on the center shelf for 30 minutes, or until the top is puffed up and browned and a knife inserted in the center of the custard comes out clean. Remove from the oven and carefully slide onto a wire rack for 5 to 10 minutes to let the custard set. Serve hot.

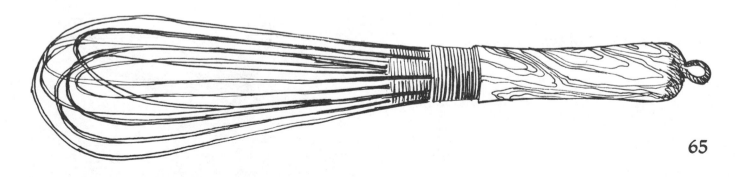

ZUCCHINI BACON QUICHE

1 pastry shell
2-1/2 cups coarsely grated, unpeeled
    zucchini (4 to 6)
Salt
4 slices bacon
1/2 cup chopped onion
1-1/2 tablespoons butter or bacon
    drippings
1 tablespoon flour
6 ounces Swiss cheese, grated
3 eggs
1-1/2 cups half-and-half
1/8 teaspoon black pepper

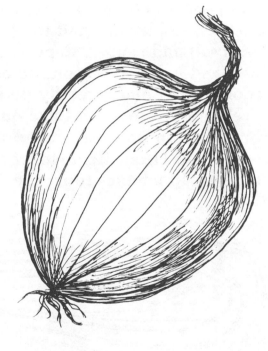

Grate the zucchini onto a piece of tinfoil and sprinkle with salt. Let stand for about 30 minutes, then squeeze out the excess moisture and dry. Cut the bacon into small pieces and fry in a heavy skillet until crisp. Remove and drain on paper towels and set aside. In the same pan in either the drippings or the butter saute the onions for 5 to 10 minutes, or until tender and golden. Stir in the flour and zucchini and heat for 1 minute. Spread half of the cheese and bacon over the bottom of the shell. Lightly beat the eggs with a wire whisk. Add the half-and-half and pepper and blend until smooth. Set the pastry shell on a cookie sheet and carefully pour in the custard mixture. Sprinkle with the rest of the cheese and bacon. Preheat oven to 400°. Bake on the center shelf of the oven for 15 minutes. Reduce the heat to 350° and bake for 20 to 25 minutes longer, or until the top is puffed up and browned and a knife inserted into the center of the custard comes out clean. Remove from the oven and carefully slide onto a wire rack for 5 to 10 minutes to let the custard set. Garnish, if desired, and serve hot.

ZUCCHINI GREEN CHILE QUICHE

1 pastry shell
3 cups coarsely grated, unpeeled
  zucchini (3/4 pound)
Salt
4 ounce can whole green chiles (do not
  use prediced)
1-1/2 tablespoons butter
3/4 cup sliced green onions
1 tablespoon flour
1/4 pound sharp Cheddar, grated
2 ounces Monterey Jack, shredded
3 eggs
1-1/2 cups half-and-half
1/8 teaspoon black pepper
1/8 teaspoon salt

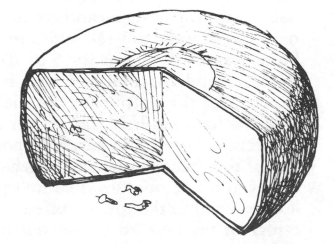

Grate the zucchini onto a piece of tin foil and sprinkle with salt. Let stand for about 30 minutes, then squeeze out all the excess moisture and dry. Rinse and seed the chiles, dry and cut into small pieces. Melt the butter in a heavy skillet and saute the green onions for about 1 minute. Stir in the zucchini and heat for several minutes. Blend in the flour. Spread over the bottom of the pastry shell. Sprinkle with half the cheese and all the chiles. Lightly beat the eggs with a wire whisk. Add the half-and-half and seasonings and blend until smooth. Set the pastry shell on a cookie sheet and carefully pour in the custard mixture. Sprinkle with the remaining cheeses. Preheat oven to 400°. Bake on the center shelf of the oven for 15 minutes. Reduce the heat to 350° and bake for 20 to 25 minutes, or until the top is puffed up and browned and a knife inserted into the center of the custard comes out clean. Remove from the oven and carefully slide onto a wire rack for 5 to 10 minutes to let the custard set. Garnish, if desired, and serve hot.

ASPARAGUS QUICHE

1 pastry shell
10 ounce package frozen asparagus
    spears
1 tablespoon butter
4 eggs
2 cups heavy cream
1/2 teaspoon salt
1/8 teaspoon black pepper

GARNISH
1 tablespoon chopped parsley
Sprinkling of paprika

Cook the asparagus according to package directions. Drain and cool. Cut each spear in half crosswise. Slice the bottom halves into small pieces. Reserve spears. Arrange the bottom pieces in the pastry shell and dot with butter. Lightly beat the eggs with a wire whisk. Add the cream and seasonings and blend until smooth. Set the pastry shell on a cookie sheet and carefully pour in the custard mixture. Preheat oven to 375°. Bake on center shelf for 10 minutes. Remove the quiche and set the asparagus tips into the custard, pointed ends up. Return to oven and bake for 5 more minutes, or until top is puffed up and browned and a knife inserted in the center of the custard comes out clean. Remove from the oven and carefully slide onto a wire rack for 5 to 10 minutes to let the custard set. Garnish and serve hot.

BROCCOLI AND CHEESE QUICHE

1 pastry shell
10 ounce package frozen chopped
    broccoli
1 cup dry breadcrumbs
4 ounces American cheese slices
2 ounce jar pimentos, drained and
    chopped
4 ounces Swiss cheese slices
4 eggs
2 cups half-and-half
1 tablespoon chopped onion
1 teaspoon salt
1/8 teaspoon black pepper
1/2 teaspoon prepared mustard
2 tablespoons butter, melted

GARNISH
1 tablespoon chopped parsley
1 pitted ripe olive, thinly sliced
Sprinkling of paprika

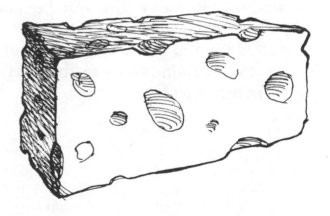

Cook the broccoli according to package directions. Drain and set aside. Spread half the breadcrumbs over the bottom of the pastry shell. Cover with torn slices of American cheese. Spread the broccoli on top, cover with the pimento, and add torn slices of Swiss cheese. Lightly beat the eggs with a wire whisk. Add the half-and-half and seasonings and blend until smooth. Set the pastry shell on a cookie sheet and carefully pour in the custard mixture. In a small bowl, combine the remaining bread crumbs and melted butter and spread over the top of the quiche. Preheat oven to 325°. Bake on the center shelf of the oven for 60 minutes, or until the top is puffed up and browned and a knife inserted in the center of the custard comes out clean. Remove from the oven and carefully slide onto a wire rack for 5 to 10 minutes to let the custard set. Garnish and serve hot.

SPICY CAULIFLOWER QUICHE

1 pastry shell
1 head fresh cauliflower
2 tablespoons butter
1 teaspoon mustard seeds
1 large onion, diced
1 large firm tomato, cut in wedges
1 cup plain yogurt
1/2 cup water
1 teaspoon ginger
1/2 teaspoon salt
1/2 teaspoon coriander
1/2 teaspoon cumin
1/4 teaspoon tumeric
1/2 teaspoon cayenne pepper
3 eggs
1/2 cup heavy cream

GARNISH
1 pimento, thinly sliced
1 green pepper, thinly sliced
1 pitted ripe olive, thinly sliced
Sprinkling of chopped parsley
Sprinkling of paprika

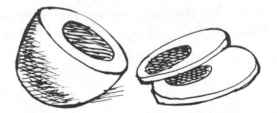

Cook the cauliflower in boiling salted water for about 10 minutes, or until tender but still firm. Cool and split into flowerets. Heat the butter in a heavy skillet and add the mustard seeds. When the seeds have popped, add the onions and saute until tender. Add the tomatoes, yogurt, water, and all seasonings except the cayenne. Bring to a boil, then reduce the heat and cook until the mixture becomes heavy and creamy. Arrange the cauliflower in the pastry shell and cover with the sauce. Sprinkle with cayenne. Beat the eggs lightly with a wire whisk. add the cream and blend until smooth. Set the pastry shell on a cookie sheet and carefully pour in the custard mixture. Preheat oven to 350°. Bake on the center shelf of the oven for 30 to 40 minutes, or until the top is puffed up and browned and a knife inserted in the center of the custard comes out clean. Remove from the oven and carefully slide onto a wire rack for 5 to 10 minutes to let the custard set. Garnish and serve hot.

CORN QUICHE

1 pastry shell
2 leeks
1/2 onion, finely chopped
2 tablespoons butter
1 tablespoon flour
1-1/2 cups heavy cream, scalded
1/4 pound sharp Cheddar cheese, grated
1 green pepper, finely chopped
2 8-ounce cans whole kernel corn
4 eggs
1/2 teaspoon salt
1/4 teaspoon black pepper

GARNISH
Several thin slices green pepper
1 teaspoon finely chopped pimento
2 pitted ripe olives, thinly sliced

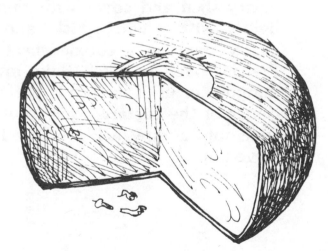

Cut the leeks into small pieces and mix with the onion. Melt the butter in a heavy skillet and saute the leeks and onions until tender. Stir in the flour, cream, and all but 2 tablespoons of the grated cheese. Mix the chopped pepper and corn and add to the leek mixture. Lightly beat the eggs, stir in the cream, and blend into the vegetables. Add the seasonings and blend until smooth. Set the pastry shell on a cookie sheet and carefully pour in the vegetable-custard mixture. Sprinkle with the remaining grated cheese. Preheat oven to 350°. Bake on the center shelf of the oven for 30 to 40 minutes, or until the top is puffed up and browned and a knife inserted in the center of the custard comes out clean. Remove from the oven and carefully slide onto a wire rack for 5 to 10 minutes to let the custard set. Garnish and serve hot.

MUSHROOM QUICHE

1 pastry shell
4 tablespoons butter
2 tablespoons chopped green onions
1 pound mushrooms, thinly sliced
1-1/2 teaspoons salt
1 teaspoon lemon juice
4 eggs
1 cup heavy cream
1/8 teaspoon black pepper
1/8 teapoon nutmeg
2 ounces Swiss cheese, grated

GARNISH
1/8 teaspoon black pepper
Sprinkling of paprika

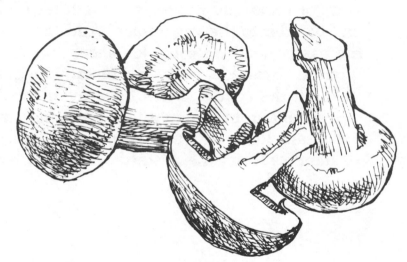

Melt the butter in a heavy skillet and add the green onions. Cook for about 1 minute, then add the sliced mushrooms, 1 teaspoon salt, and lemon juice. Cover the pan and simmer over a low heat for about 10 minutes. Remove the cover, bring to a boil, and cook for 5 to 10 minutes, or until the liquid has evaporated. Continue cooking for 2 to 3 minutes more, stirring constantly to keep the mushrooms from sticking. Lightly beat the eggs with a wire whisk. Add the cream, pepper, and nutmeg. Stir in the mushroom mixture. Set the pastry shell on a cookie sheet and carefully pour in the vegetable-custard mixture. Sprinkle with the grated cheese. Preheat oven to 350°. Bake on the center shelf of the oven for 35 minutes, or until the top is puffed up and browned and a knife inserted in the center of the custard comes out clean. Remove from the oven and carefully slide onto a wire rack for 5 to 10 minutes to let the custard set. Garnish and serve hot.

MUSHROOM AND BACON QUICHE

1 pastry shell
1/4 pound bacon
2 tablespoons butter
1/2 pound mushrooms, thinly sliced
6 ounces Swiss cheese grated
1/4 cup grated Parmesan cheese
3 eggs
2 cups heavy cream, scalded
1/4 teaspoon salt
1/8 teaspoon black pepper
1/8 teaspoon nutmeg
2 tablespoons breadcrumbs

GARNISH
Several parsley sprigs, plus
  1 teaspoon finely chopped parsley
1 whole pimento cut into long slivers
Sprinkling of paprika

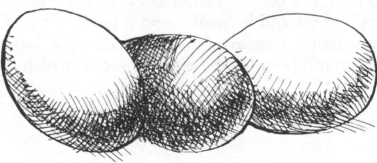

Cut the bacon into small pieces and saute until crisp in a heavy skillet. Remove and drain on paper towels and set aside. Melt the butter and saute the mushrooms. Add the bacon and the grated cheese to the mushrooms. Add the bacon and the grated cheese to the mushrooms. Lightly beat the eggs with a wire whisk. Add the cream and seasonings and beat until smooth. Set the pastry shell on a cookie sheet. Sprinkle with the breadcrumbs. Spread the bottom of the shell evenly with the mushroom mixture. Carefully pour in the custard mixture. Preheat oven to 425°. Bake on the center shelf of the oven for 10 minutes. Reduce the heat to 350° and bake for 20 to 25 minutes longer, or until the top is puffed up and browned and a knife inserted in the center of the custard comes out clean. Remove from the oven and carefully slide onto a wire rack for 5 to 10 minutes to let the custard set. Garnish and serve hot.

SAVORY POTATO QUICHE

1 pastry shell
3 tablespoons butter
2 large potatoes, baked
   and cut into thin slices
1/2 cup grated Parmesan cheese
4 eggs
2 cups half-and-half
1/2 teaspoon seasoned salt
1/2 teaspoon summer savory
1/2 teaspoon dry mustard
1/8 teaspoon cayenne pepper

GARNISH
1 tablespoon chopped parsley
Sprinkling of paprika

Melt the butter in a heavy skillet over a low heat. Add the potato slices and saute until coated with butter and slightly brown. Using about 3 tablespoons of the grated cheese, dust each potato slice on both sides and arrange the slices in the pastry shell. Lightly beat the eggs with a wire whisk. Add the half-and-half and seasonings and blend until smooth. Set the pastry shell on a cookie sheet and carefully pour in the custard mixture. Sprinkle with the remaining grated cheese. Preheat oven to 375°. Bake on the center shelf of the oven for 30 minutes, or until the top is puffed up and browned and a knife inserted in the center of the custard comes out clean. Remove from the oven and carefully slide onto a wire rack for 5 to 10 minutes to let the custard set. Garnish and serve hot.

SPINACH NOODLE MUSHROOM QUICHE

1 pastry shell
3/4 pound spinach noodles
2 tablespoons butter
3 cups sliced mushrooms
1 onion, chopped
1/4 cup sliced ripe olives
3 eggs
2 small cans evaporated milk
2 teaspoons salt
1/2 teaspoon white pepper
1/2 teaspoon nutmeg
3/4 cup bread crumbs
1/4 pound Swiss cheese, grated
1/2 cup grated Parmesan cheese

GARNISH
1 pimento, thinly sliced
2 stuffed green olives, sliced thin

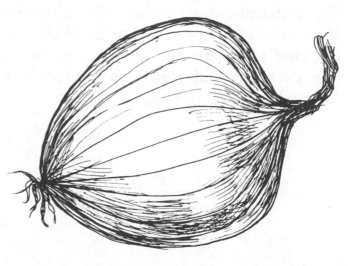

Cook the noodles in boiling salted water for 5 to 7 minutes, or just until tender but firm. Drain and set aside. Melt butter in a heavy skillet and saute the mushrooms and onions until tender. Add the olives and noodles. Lightly beat the eggs with a wire whisk. Add the evaporated milk and seasonings and blend until smooth. Spread 1/2 cup of the crumbs over the bottom of the pastry shell. Slowly pour in half the noodle mixture. Over this, sprinkle half the grated Swiss cheese. Add the remaining noodle mixture. Set the pastry shell on a cookie sheet and carefully pour in the custard mixture. Sprinkle with the remaining crumbs, Swiss cheese, and Parmesan cheese. Preheat oven to 350°. Bake on the center shelf of the oven for 30 to 35 minutes, or until the top is puffed up and browned and a knife inserted in the center of the custard comes out clean. Remove from the oven and carefully slide onto a wire rack for 5 to 10 minutes to let the custard set. Garnish and serve hot.

VERMICELLI QUICHE

1 pastry shell
1/2 pound vermicelli, broken in half
2 tablespoons butter
1 green pepper, chopped
1 onion, chopped
3 eggs
1 cup milk
1 cup sour cream
2 tablespoons chopped chives
2 teaspoons salt
1/2 teaspoon white pepper
1/2 teaspoon paprika
1/4 pound Monterey Jack cheese, grated
2/3 cup dry breadcrumbs

GARNISH
Several parsley sprigs
1 large mushroom, thinly sliced
1 pitted, ripe olive, thinly sliced

Cook vermicelli in boiling salted water 5 to 6 minutes, or just until tender but firm. Melt the butter in a heavy skillet, add the green pepper and onion, and saute until tender. Lightly beat the eggs with a wire whisk. Add the milk and sour cream and blend until smooth. Add the onions, green peppers, chives and seasonings and half the grated cheese. Slowly fold in the vermicelli. Set the pastry shell on a cookie sheet and sprinkle with half the breadcrumbs. Carefully pour in the pasta-custard mixture and top with the remaining crumbs and grated cheese. Preheat oven to 350°. Bake on the center shelf of the oven for 40 to 50 minutes, or until the top is puffed up and browned and a knife inserted in the center of the custard comes out clean. Remove from the oven and carefully slide onto a wire rack for 5 to 10 minutes to let the custard set. Garnish and serve hot.

SPINACH QUICHE

1 pastry shell
10 ounce package frozen chopped
  spinach
2 tablespoons butter
1 cup finely chopped onion
1/2 cup finely chopped celery
1 garlic clove, finely chopped
1/2 teaspoon salt
1/8 teaspoon white pepper
2 eggs
2 egg yolks
1-1/2 cups half-and-half, scalded
1 teaspoon Dijon mustard
1/8 teaspoon cayenne pepper
1/8 teaspoon nutmeg
1 package frozen onion rings

GARNISH
1 pimento, thinly sliced
1 chile pepper, thinly sliced
1 pitted ripe olive, thinly sliced
1 wedge Gruyere cheese, thinly sliced

Cook frozen spinach according to package directions, drain and dry thoroughly, pressing into a sieve to remove excess moisture. Set aside. Melt the butter in a heavy skillet. Add the onion, celery, and garlic. Saute 3 to 4 minutes, then add the spinach and the salt and pepper. Lightly beat the eggs and yolks with a wire whisk. Add the half-and-half and seasonings and blend until smooth. Add the spinach mixture and blend thoroughly. Set the pastry shell on a cookie sheet and carefully pour in the spinach-custard mixture. Prepare the frozen onion rings according to package directions and set aside. Preheat oven to 350°. Bake on the center shelf of the oven for 30 to 40 minutes, or until the top is puffed up and browned and a knife inserted in the center of the custard comes out clean. Remove from the oven, arrange the onion rings on top, and return to the oven for 5 minutes, or until the onions are heated through. Remove from the oven and garnish and serve hot.

SPINACH AND CHEESE QUICHE

1 pastry shell
10 ounce package frozen chopped
   spinach
1/4 teaspoon salt
1/8 teaspoon black pepper
1 tablespoon horseradish
4 tablespoons sour cream
2 ounces Swiss cheese, grated
3 tablespoons grated Parmesan cheese
4 eggs
1-1/2 cups half-and-half
1/8 teaspoon salt
1/8 teaspoon cayenne pepper
1/8 teaspoon nutmeg

GARNISH
1 chile, cut in strips
1 pimento, cut in strips
2 pitted ripe olives, thinly sliced
Sprinkling of paprika

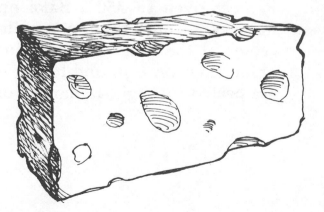

Cook the spinach according to package directions. Drain and dry thoroughly, pressing into a sieve to remove excess moisture. Place in a bowl and blend in salt, pepper, horseradish, and sour cream. Spread the mixture in the pastry shell. Sprinkle with the grated cheeses. Lightly beat the eggs with a wire whisk. Add the half-and-half, and seasonings and blend until smooth. Set the pastry shell on a cookie sheet and carefully pour in the custard mixture. Preheat oven to 375°. Bake on the center shelf of the oven for 40 minutes, or until the top is puffed up and browned and a knife inserted in the center of the custard comes out clean. Remove from the oven and carefully slide onto a wire rack for 5 to 10 minutes to let the custard set. Garnish and serve hot.

SPINACH AND ANCHOVY QUICHE

1 pastry shell
10 ounce package frozen chopped
   spinach
2 ounces anchovy fillets, drained
2 hardboiled eggs, sliced
1/4 pound Swiss cheese, grated
4 eggs
1-1/2 cups half-and-half, scalded
1/4 teaspoon nutmeg
1/4 teaspoon black pepper

GARNISH
Several parsley sprigs
Sprinkling of paprika

Cook the spinach according to package directions. Drain and dry thoroughly, pressing into a sieve to remove excess moisture. Spread half the spinach over the bottom of the pastry shell, cover with half the anchovies, then half the sliced eggs. Sprinkle with half the grated cheese. Repeat. Lightly beat the eggs with a wire whisk. Add the half-and-half and seasonings and blend until smooth. Set the pastry shell on a cookie sheet and carefully pour in the custard mixture. Preheat the oven to 375°. Bake on the center shelf of the oven for 35 minutes, or until the top is puffed up and browned and a knife inserted in the center of the custard comes out clean. Remove from the oven and carefully slide onto a wire rack for 5 to 10 minutes to let the custard set. Garnish and serve hot.

CHILE QUICHE

1 pastry shell
4 ounce can diced green chiles, drained
1/2 cup chopped black olives
1/3 cup pimentos, thinly sliced
3 tablespoons butter
1 tablespoon flour
1 cup half-and-half
3 eggs
3/4 teaspoon salt
1/8 teaspoon black pepper
1/8 teaspoon nutmeg
2 ounces mozzarella cheese, grated
2 ounces mild Cheddar cheese, grated

GARNISH
Several parsley sprigs
Sprinkling of paprika

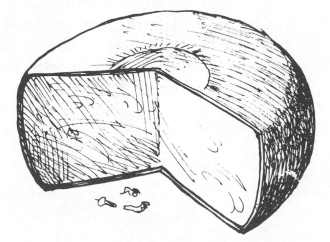

94

Spread the chiles, chopped olives, and pimentos over the bottom of the pastry shell. Melt the butter in a heavy skillet, stir in the flour, and beat in the half-and-half with a wire whisk. Beat the eggs with whisk and blend them into the mixture. Add the seasonings and blend until smooth. Stir in the grated cheeses. Set the pastry shell on a cookie sheet and carefully pour in the vegetable-custard mixture. Preheat oven to 375°. Bake on the center shelf of the oven for 25 to 30 minutes, or until the top is puffed up and browned and a knife inserted in the center of the custard comes out clean. Remove from the oven and carefully slide onto a wire rack for 5 to 10 minutes to let the custard set. Garnish and serve hot.

CHRISTMAS QUICHE

1 pastry shell
2 large green peppers, cut into wide strips
2 large red peppers, cut into wide strips
4 ounces anchovy fillets, drained
1 cup seasoned stuffing mix
1/4 pound Swiss cheese, grated
4 eggs
1-1/2 cups half-and-half, scalded
1/8 teaspoon cayenne pepper
1/8 teaspoon black pepper

GARNISH
Several parsley sprigs
1 pitted ripe olive, thinly sliced
Sprinkling of paprika

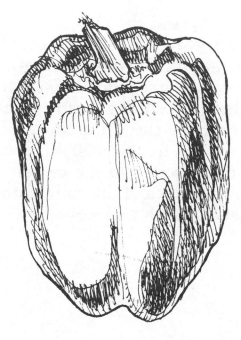

Spread the bottom of the pastry shell with pepper slices. Place the anchovies on top of the peppers. Sprinkle the stuffing mix over the anchovies and peppers. Sprinkle the grated cheese over all. Lightly beat the eggs with a wire whisk. Add the half-and-half and seasonings and blend until smooth. Set the pastry shell on a cookie sheet and carefully pour in the custard mixture. Preheat oven to 350°. Bake on the center shelf of the oven for 30 to 40 minutes, or until the top is puffed up and browned and a knife inserted in the center of the custard comes out clean. Remove from the oven and carefully slide onto a wire rack for 5 to 10 minutes to let the custard set. Garnish and serve hot.

QUICHE ST. TROPEZ

1 pastry shell
1 onion, chopped
1 green pepper, chopped
2 tablespoons butter
4 small firm tomatoes, thinly sliced
2 tablespoons flour
1 teaspoon thyme
2 ounces Swiss cheese, grated
3 eggs
1 cup half-and-half
1/4 teaspoon salt
1/4 teaspoon black pepper
2 tablespoons breadcrumbs
1/4 teaspoon nutmeg

GARNISH
3 thin slices green pepper
3 firm small tomatoes, halved

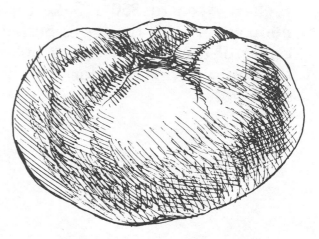

In a heavy skillet, cook the onion and green pepper in 1 tablespoon of the butter until tender. Remove the vegetables from the skillet. Dust the tomatoes with the flour, add the remaining butter to the skillet, and saute the tomatoes 3 to 5 minutes. Arrange the tomatoes in the pastry shell, sprinkle with thyme, and cover with the onions and green pepper. Sprinkle with the grated cheese. Lightly beat the eggs with a wire whisk. Add the half-and-half and seasonings and blend until smooth. Set the pastry shell on a cookie sheet and carefully pour in the custard mixture. Sprinkle with breadcrumbs and nutmeg. Preheat oven to 375°. Bake on center shelf of the oven for 35 minutes, or until the top is puffed up and browned and a knife inserted in the center of the custard comes out clean. Remove from the oven and carefully slide onto a wire rack for 5 to 10 minutes to let the custard set. Garnish and serve hot.

Meat
Quiches

QUICHE LORRAINE HENRI

1 pastry shell
10 slices Canadian bacon
8 ounces Swiss cheese, grated
4 eggs
2 cups half-and-half
Pinch cayenne
Pinch nutmeg
1/4 teaspoon salt

GARNISH
Several parsley sprigs

Saute the bacon in a heavy skillet until browned on both sides, drain, and cut into small pieces. Spread the bacon over the bottom of the pastry shell. Sprinkle the cheese over the bacon. Lightly beat the eggs with a wire whisk. Add the half-and-half and seasonings and blend until smooth. Set the pastry shell on a cookie sheet and carefully pour in the custard mixture. Preheat oven to 375°. Bake on the center shelf of the oven for 35 to 40 minutes, or until the top is puffed up and browned and a knife inserted into the center of the custard comes out clean. Remove from the oven and carefully slide onto a wire rack for 5 to 10 minutes to let the custard set. Garnish and serve hot.

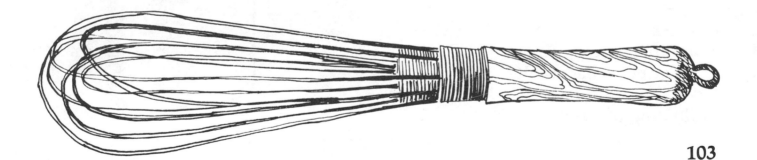

QUICHE ALSACE LORRAINE

1 pastry shell
1/2 pound bacon
2 onions, chopped
3 eggs
1 cup sour cream
1 cup half-and-half
1 tablespoon chopped chives
1/2 teaspoon salt
1/4 teaspoon black pepper
2 teaspoons caraway seeds

GARNISH
1 hardboiled egg, grated
1/2 teaspoon bacon bits
Several parsley sprigs
Sprinkling of paprika

Cut the bacon into small pieces and fry in a heavy skillet until crisp. Remove and drain on paper towels and set aside. Saute the onions for 5 to 10 minutes in the remaining fat. Lightly beat the eggs with a wire whisk. Add the sour cream, half-and-half, chives, salt and pepper and blend until smooth. Add the bacon and onion and mix well. Set the pastry shell on a cookie sheet and carefully pour in the filling mixture. Sprinkle with caraway seeds. Preheat oven to 350°. Bake on the center shelf for 30 to 40 minutes, or until the top is puffed up and browned and a knife inserted in the center of the custard comes out clean. Remove from the oven and carefully slide onto a wire rack for 5 to 10 minutes to let the custard set. Garnish and serve hot.

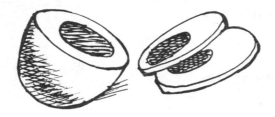

BACON AND MUSHROOM QUICHE

1 pastry shell
1/2 pound bacon
3 tablespoons butter
1/2 pound mushrooms, thinly sliced
1/2 teaspoon salt
1/8 teaspoon black pepper
2 tablespoons chopped parsley
2 eggs
1 cup half-and-half
1/8 teaspoon salt
1/8 teaspoon cayenne pepper
1/8 teaspoon nutmeg

GARNISH
Several parsley sprigs

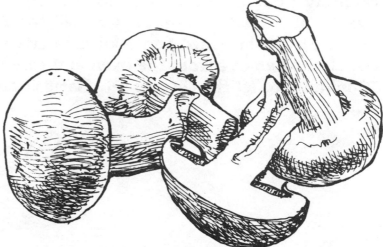

Cut the bacon into small pieces and fry in a heavy skillet until crisp. Remove and drain on paper towels and set aside. Melt the butter in a heavy skillet and cook the mushrooms over a moderate heat until their liquid content has evaporated. Season with salt, pepper, and parsley. Add the bacon, mix well, and spread in the pastry shell. Lightly beat the eggs with a wire whisk. Add the half-and-half and seasonings and blend until smooth. Set the pastry shell on a cookie sheet and carefully pour in the custard mixture. Preheat oven to 375°. Bake on the center shelf for 40 minutes, or until the top is puffed up and browned and a knife inserted in the center of the custard comes out clean. Remove from the oven and carefully slide onto a wire rack for 5 to 10 minutes to let the custard set. Garnish and serve hot.

BACON AND VEAL QUICHE

1 pastry shell
1/2 pound bacon
1/2 pound veal
1 tablespoon flour
3 hardboiled eggs, sliced
4 eggs
1-1/2 cups heavy cream
1/4 teaspoon marjoram
1/2 teaspoon thyme
1/4 cup chopped parsley

GARNISH
1/4 teaspoon black pepper
1/4 teaspoon nutmeg
1/4 teaspoon paprika
Several parsley sprigs

108

Cut the bacon into small pieces and fry in a heavy skillet until crisp. Remove and drain on paper towels and set aside. Cube veal, dust with flour, and saute for 10 minutes in remaining bacon fat. Spread veal, bacon, and hardboiled eggs over the bottom of the pastry shell. Lightly beat the eggs with a wire whisk. Add the cream and seasonings and blend until smooth. Set the pastry shell on a cookie sheet and carefully pour in the custard mixture. Preheat oven to 375°. Bake on the center shelf of the oven for 35 minutes, or until the top is puffed up and browned and a knife inserted in the center of the custard comes out clean. Remove from the oven and carefully slide onto a wire rack for 5 to 10 minutes to let the custard set. Garnish and serve hot.

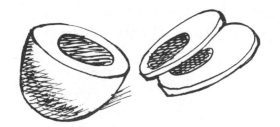

HAM QUICHE

1 pastry shell
1/2 pound cooked ham, diced (or bacon)
1/4 pound Swiss cheese, grated
4 eggs
1-1/2 cups half-and-half
1 ounce sherry
1/8 teaspoon salt
1/8 teaspoon cayenne pepper
1/8 teaspoon nutmeg

GARNISH
2 tablespoons chopped chives
2 stuffed green olives, thinly sliced

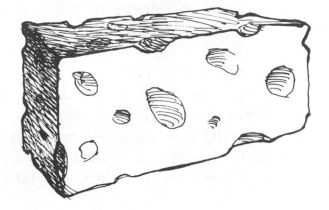

110

Spread the ham over the bottom of the pastry shell and cover with the grated cheese. Lightly beat the eggs with a wire whisk. Add the half-and-half, sherry, and seasonings and blend until smooth. Set the pastry shell on a cookie sheet and carefully pour in the custard mixture. Preheat oven to 375°. Bake on the center shelf for 40 minutes, or until the top is puffed up and browned and a knife inserted in the center of the custard comes out clean. Remove from the oven and carefully slide onto a wire rack for 5 to 10 minutes to let the custard set. Garnish and serve hot.

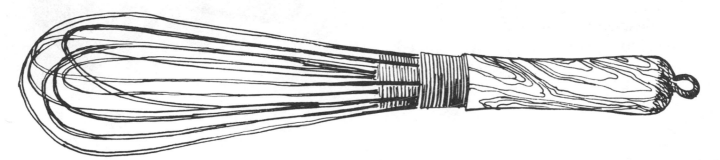

HAM AND CHEESE QUICHE

1 pastry shell
1 cup diced cooked ham
2 ounces Cheddar cheese, grated
2 ounces Swiss cheese, grated
4 eggs
1-1/2 cups heavy cream
1/2 teaspoon salt
1/4 teaspoon black pepper

GARNISH
2 tablespoons chopped chives
2 stuffed green olives, thinly sliced

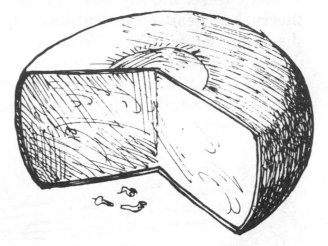

Spread the diced ham over the bottom of the pastry shell. Sprinkle with about half the cheeses, reserving several tablespoons of each cheese for the top of the quiche. Lightly beat the eggs with a wire whisk. Add the cream and seasonings and blend until smooth. Set the pastry shell on a cookie sheet and carefully pour in the custard mixture. Sprinkle with the reserved cheeses. Preheat oven to 375°. Bake on the center shelf of the oven for 30 minutes, or until the top is puffed up and browned and a knife inserted in the center of the custard comes out clean. Remove from the oven and carefully slide onto a wire rack for 5 to 10 minutes to let the custard set. Garnish and serve hot.

HAM AND POTATO QUICHE

1 pastry shell
2 potatoes, peeled
2 onions, chopped
1 large green pepper, chopped
3/4 pound cooked ham, diced
3 eggs
1-1/2 cups half-and-half
1/4 teaspoon salt
1/8 teaspoon black pepper
2 tablespoons grated Parmesan cheese

GARNISH
1 tablespoon chopped parsley
Sprinkling of paprika

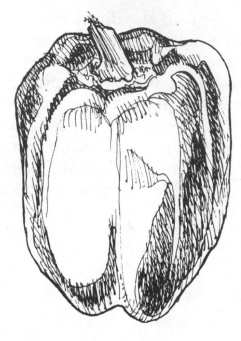

Boil the potatoes in salted water for about 10 minutes. Cool and cut in slices. Spread half the potato slices over the bottom of the pastry shell. Sprinkle half the vegetables over the potatoes. Cover with half the diced ham. Repeat. Lightly beat the eggs with a wire whisk. Add the half-and-half and seasonings and blend until smooth. Set the pastry shell on a cookie sheet and carefully pour in the custard mixture. Preheat oven to 350°. Bake on the center shelf of the oven for 30 minutes, or until top is puffed up and browned and a knife inserted in the center of the custard comes out clean. Remove from the oven and sprinkle the grated Parmesan cheese over the top. Place under the broiler until the cheese melts and turns golden brown. Remove and carefully slide onto a wire rack for 5 to 10 minutes. Garnish and serve hot.

QUICHE MAISON EDIE

1 pastry shell
1/4 pound prosciutto
1/4 pound Gruyere cheese
4 eggs
2 cups half-and-half
1 tablespoon dried onion flakes
1/8 teaspoon black pepper
1/8 teaspoon cayenne pepper
1/8 teaspoon nutmeg

GARNISH
Several parsley sprigs
A sprinkling of nutmeg

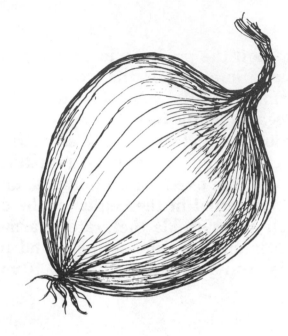

Tear the prosciutto into small pieces. Cut the cheese into pieces about the same size. Spread the ham and cheese over the bottom of the pastry shell. Lightly beat the eggs with a wire whisk. Add the half-and-half, onion flakes, and seasonings and blend until smooth. Set the pastry shell on a cookie sheet and carefully pour in the custard mixture. Preheat oven to 350°. Bake on the center shelf of the oven for 30 minutes, or until the top is puffed and browned and a knife inserted in the center of the custard comes out clean. Remove from the oven and carefully slide onto a wire rack for 5 to 10 minutes to let the custard set. Garnish and serve hot.

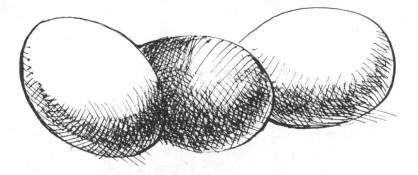

SAUSAGE AND LEEK QUICHE

1 pastry shell
1/2 cup butter
1-1/2 pounds leeks, finely chopped
2 egg yolks
1/2 cup heavy cream
1/2 teaspoon salt
1/8 teaspoon black pepper
1 green pepper, cut into strips
3 tablespoons butter
8 country-style sausages, cooked and
   sliced

GARNISH
Sprinkling of paprika

In a heavy skillet, melt half the butter and add the leeks. Cover and cook over a low heat for 20 minutes, or until the leeks are very tender. Remove the leeks and set aside to cool. Saute the green pepper strips in the butter. Beat the egg yolks with a wire whisk. Add the cream and seasonings and blend until smooth. Add the leeks. Set the pastry shell on a cookie sheet and carefully pour in the leek-custard mixture. Arrange the sausage slices on top of the quiche and add the green peppers. Preheat oven to 375°. Bake on the center shelf of the oven for 30 minutes, or until the top is puffed up and browned and a knife inserted in the center of the custard comes out clean. Remove from the oven and carefully slide onto a wire rack for 5 to 10 minutes to let the custard set. Garnish and serve hot.

ITALIAN SAUSAGE AND CHEESE QUICHE

1 pastry shell
1/3 cup grated Parmesan cheese
1/8 teaspoon paprika
3/4 pound sweet Italian sausage
2/3 cup ricotta cheese
1/4 teaspoon salt
1/8 teaspoon black pepper
3 tablespoons chopped parsley
4 eggs
1-1/2 cups half-and-half
1/8 teaspoon salt
1/8 teaspoon cayenne pepper
1/8 teaspoon nutmeg

GARNISH
Thin strips of pimento
Thin strips of chile pepper
1 pitted ripe olive, thinly sliced

If you are preparing a shell especially for this recipe, add the Parmesan cheese and paprika to the dough during mixing. Otherwise, sprinkle the grated Parmesan cheese and paprika over the shell. Remove the sausage meat from the casings, crumble, and cook in a heavy skillet over a low heat until cooked but not brown. Pour off the excess fat and stir in the ricotta, salt, pepper, and parsley. Remove from the heat. Beat the eggs lightly with a wire whisk. Add the half-and-half and seasonings and blend until smooth. Stir the sausage-cheese mixture into the custard and blend. Set the pastry shell on a cookie sheet and carefully pour in the filling mixture. Preheat oven to 400°. Bake on the center shelf of the oven for 40 to 45 minutes, or until the top is puffed up and browned and a knife inserted in the center of the custard comes out clean. Remove from the oven and carefully slide onto a wire rack for 5 to 10 minutes to let the custard set. Garnish and serve hot.

CHEDDAR LINKS QUICHE

1 pastry shell
12 ounces pork sausage links
1 onion, thinly sliced
1 green pepper, chopped
6 ounces sharp Cheddar cheese, grated
1 tablespoon flour
2 eggs
1 cup heavy cream
1 tablespoon parsley flakes
3/4 teaspoon seasoned salt
1/4 teaspoon garlic salt
1/4 teaspoon black pepper

GARNISH
1 tablespoon chopped chives
Sprinkling of paprika

Fry the sausages until fully cooked. Drain on paper towels. Reserve 2 tablespoons of fat. Cook the onion and green pepper in the fat for 2 to 3 minutes. Slice the sausages into thin pieces. In a large bowl, mix together the cheese and flour. Gently stir in the sausage, onions, and green pepper. Spread this mixture in the pastry shell. Lightly beat the eggs with a wire whisk. Add the cream and seasonings and blend until smooth. Set the pastry shell on a cookie sheet and carefully pour in the custard mixture. Preheat oven to 375°. Bake on the center shelf for 35 to 40 minutes, or until the top is puffed up and browned and a knife inserted in the center of the custard comes out clean. Remove from the oven and carefully slide onto a wire rack for 5 to 10 minutes to let the custard set. Garnish and serve hot.

MEAT AND CHEESE QUICHE

1 pastry shell
1 pound lean ground beef
1 green pepper, chopped
2 eggs
1/2 cup half-and-half
1/2 cup water
6 ounce can tomato paste
1/2 ounce package dry spaghetti sauce
    mix
1/3 cup grated Parmesan cheese
6 ounces mozzarella cheese, grated
1 tablespoon chopped onion

GARNISH
Several parsley sprigs
1 stuffed green olive, thinly sliced

124

Brown the ground beef in a heavy skillet. Drain off the excess fat and add the green pepper, and cook 2 to 3 minutes longer. Lightly beat the eggs with a wire whisk. Add the half-and-half and blend thoroughly. Add the water, tomato paste and spaghetti sauce mix and blend until smooth. Stir this mixture into the ground beef, cover the skillet, and simmer for 10 minutes over a low heat. Sprinkle half the grated Parmesan cheese over the pastry shell. Set the shell on a cookie sheet and carefully pour in half the meat-custard mixture. Sprinkle with two-thirds of the mozzarella cheese. Pour in the remaining meat-custard mixture and sprinkle with the remaining Parmesan cheese. Preheat oven to 400°. Bake on the center shelf of the oven for 15 minutes. Remove from the oven, sprinkle on the remaining mozzarella cheese and raw onion, and return to oven for 3 to 5 minutes, or until the cheese melts. Remove and carefully slide onto a wire rack for 5 to 10 minutes. Garnish and serve hot.

BEEF AND ONION QUICHE

1 pastry shell
4 eggs
1 cup heavy cream
2 cups seasoned stuffing mix
1/2 pound ground beef
1 cup sliced green onions
1 teaspoon Worcestershire sauce
1/4 teaspoon salt
1/8 teaspoon paprika
1/8 teaspoon black pepper
1/4 pound sharp Cheddar cheese, grated
4 dashes Tabasco sauce
Sprinkling of paprika

GARNISH
12 slices cucumber pickle
Sprinkling of dill seeds

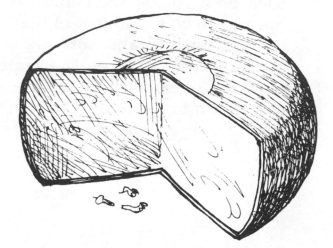

126

Lightly beat one egg with a wire whisk. Add 1/2 cup cream and the stuffing mix. Set aside until most of the cream and egg mixture is absorbed. Add the ground beef, half of the onion, and the seasonings and mix only until combined. Spoon evenly into the pastry shell. Sprinkle with the remaining onion. Beat 3 eggs lightly with a wire whisk. Stir in the grated cheese, Tabasco sauce, and the rest of the heavy cream. Set the pastry shell on a cookie sheet and carefully pour in the custard mixture. Sprinkle the top with paprika. Preheat oven to 375°. Bake on the center shelf of the oven for 35 minutes, or until the top is puffed up and browned and a knife inserted into the center of the custard comes out clean. Remove from the oven and carefully slide onto a wire rack for 5 to 10 minutes to let the custard set. Garnish and serve hot.

CURRIED QUICHE

1 pastry shell
1-1/2 tablespoons olive oil
1/2 cup finely chopped onion
1 garlic clove, crushed
1 teaspoon allspice
1/2 teaspoon salt
3 tablespoons curry powder
8 ounce can apricots, drained
1/2 cup prunes, soaked and drained
1/2 cup mango chutney
2 tablespoons lemon juice
1-1/2 cups cubed cooked lamb, beef,
   pork, veal, chicken, turkey, fowl,
   or fish
2 eggs
1 cup half-and-half

Several parsley sprigs

Heat the olive oil in a heavy skillet and saute the onions, garlic, allspice, and salt for 5 to 10 minutes, or until the onions are tender and golden. Add the curry powder and cook for 3 to 4 more minutes. Stir in the fruit, chutney, and lemon juice and simmer for 30 minutes, stirring frequently. Stir in the cooked meat or fish and cook for another 5 minutes. Set the pastry shell on a cookie sheet and pour in the curry mixture. Lightly beat the eggs, pour in the half-and-half, and blend until smooth. Carefully pour the custard mixture into the shell. Preheat oven to 350°. Bake on the center shelf of the oven for 30 minutes, or until the top is puffed up and browned and a knife inserted in the center of the custard comes out clean. Remove from the oven and carefully slide onto a wire rack for 5 to 10 minutes to let the custard set. Garnish and serve hot.

LAMB AND ARTICHOKE QUICHE

1 pastry shell
1-1/2 cups diced cooked lamb
1/4 pound artichoke bottoms, drained
  and diced
4 eggs
1-1/2 cups heavy cream
1/4 cup white wine
1/4 teaspoon ginger
Juice of 1 lemon
1/2 teaspoon salt
1/4 teaspoon black pepper

GARNISH
Several sprigs fresh mint
1/2 teaspoon nutmeg
Sprinkling of paprika

130

Spread the lamb and artichoke over the bottom of the pastry shell. Lightly beat the eggs with a wire whisk. Add the cream, wine, ginger, lemon juice, and seasonings and blend until smooth. Set the pastry shell on a cookie sheet and carefully pour in the custard mixture. Preheat oven to 375°. Bake on the center shelf for 35 minutes, or until the top is puffed up and browned and a knife inserted in the center of the custard comes out clean. Remove from the oven and carefully slide onto a wire rack for 5 to 10 minutes to let the custard set. Garnish and serve hot.

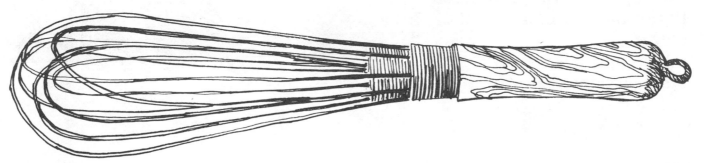

CHICKEN AND ALMOND QUICHE

1 pastry shell
1 chicken breast,
  cooked and diced or shredded
1/4 teaspoon salt
1/8 teaspoon black pepper
4 ounce can button mushrooms, drained
5 ounce can water chestnuts,
  drained and sliced
1 cup blanched almonds, chopped
1/2 cup finely chopped onion
1 teaspoon paprika
3 eggs
1-1/2 cups half-and-half
2 tablespoons sherry or dry wine

GARNISH
Several parsley sprigs
2 pitted ripe olives, thinly sliced
Sprinkling of paprika

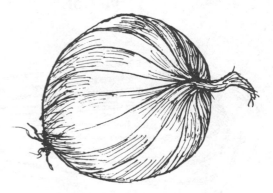

Sprinkle the diced meat with salt and pepper. Cover the bottom of the shell with half the meat, then half the mushrooms, water chestnuts, almonds, and onion. Sprinkle with paprika. Repeat. Lightly beat the eggs with a wire whisk. Add the half-and-half and blend until smooth. Stir in the wine. Set the pastry shell on a cookie sheet and carefully pour in the custard mixture. Preheat oven to 375°. Bake on the center shelf of the oven for 35 minutes, or until the top is puffed up and browned and a knife inserted in the center of the custard comes out clean. Remove from the oven and carefully slide onto a wire rack for 5 to 10 minutes to let the custard set. Garnish and serve hot.

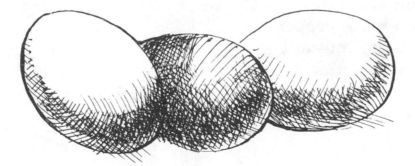

CHICKEN AND BROCCOLI QUICHE

1 pastry shell
10 ounce package frozen chopped
    broccoli
1 chicken breast,
    cooked and shredded or sliced
1/4 pound Swiss cheese, grated
3 eggs
1-1/2 cups half-and-half
1/2 teaspoon lemon juice
1/2 teaspoon salt
1/4 teaspoon black pepper
1/2 teaspoon dry mustard

GARNISH
1 hardboiled egg, grated
Several parsley sprigs
1 pitted ripe olive, thinly sliced
Sprinkling of nutmeg
Sprinkling of paprika

Cook the broccoli according to package directions. Drain and dry thoroughly, pressing into a sieve to remove excess moisture. Spread half the chicken over the bottom of the pastry shell. Cover with half the broccoli and sprinkle with half the cheese. Repeat. Lightly beat the eggs with a wire whisk. Add the half-and-half, lemon juice, and seasonings and blend until smooth. Set the pastry shell on a cookie sheet and carefully pour in the custard mixture. Preheat oven to 375°. Bake on the center shelf of the oven for 40 minutes, or until the top is puffed up and browned and a knife inserted in the center of the custard comes out clean. Remove from the oven and carefully slide onto a wire rack for 5 to 10 minutes to let the custard set. Garnish and serve hot.

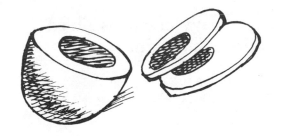

CHICKEN AND WATER CHESTNUT QUICHE

1 pastry shell
2 chicken breasts
   cooked and diced or shredded
1 teaspoon finely chopped onion
1/4 teaspoon seasoned salt
1/4 teaspoon white pepper
1/4 teaspoon poultry seasoning
1/4 teaspoon Beau Monde seasoning
1/4 teaspoon nutmeg
5 ounce can water chestnuts,
   drained and chopped
4 eggs
1-1/2 cups heavy cream, scalded
1/4 cup dry white wine

GARNISH
2 ounces Swiss cheese, grated
1/4 teaspoon paprika

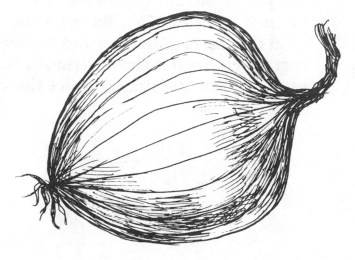

136

Place the chicken in a small bowl and mix with the onion and seasonings. Spread the chicken mixture over the bottom of the pastry shell. Sprinkle the water chestnuts over the chicken. Lightly beat the eggs with a wire whisk. Add the cream and white wine and blend until smooth. Set the pastry shell on a cookie sheet and carefully pour in the custard mixture. Preheat oven to 350°. Bake on the center shelf of the oven for 30 minutes, or until top is puffed up and browned and a knife inserted in the center of the custard comes out clean. Remove from the oven, garnish with cheese and paprika, and place under the broiler long enough to melt the cheese. Remove and carefully slide onto a wire rack for 5 to 10 minutes. Serve hot.

CHICKEN LIVER QUICHE

1 pastry shell
2 tablespoons butter
1 onion, thinly sliced
1/2 pound chicken livers
1/2 cup dry white wine
1/2 teaspoon salt
1/4 teaspoon black pepper
4 eggs
1-1/2 cups half-and-half

GARNISH
Yolk of 1 hardboiled egg, grated
1 tablespoon chopped parsley
Sprinkling of paprika

Heat the butter in a heavy skillet and saute the onions and chicken livers for 5 to 10 minutes or until the onions are tender and golden. Heat the wine in a saucepan. Add the heated wine, salt, and pepper to the chicken livers and onions. Cook for 3 minutes and set aside to cool. Lightly beat the eggs with a wire whisk. Add the half-and-half and blend until smooth. Drain the liver-onion mixture and spoon into the shell. Set the pastry shell on a cookie sheet and carefully pour in the custard mixture. Preheat oven to 350°. Bake on the center shelf of the oven for 35 minutes, or until the top is puffed up and browned and a knife inserted in the center of the custard comes out clean. Remove from the oven and carefully slide onto a wire rack for 5 to 10 minutes to let the custard set. Garnish and serve hot.

Seafood Quiches

ANCHOVY AND TOMATO QUICHE

1 pastry shell
4 medium firm tomatoes, peeled,
  seeded, and thinly sliced
2 tablespoons grated onion
2 tablespoons dried basil
2 ounces anchovy fillets, drained
4 eggs
2 cups half-and-half
1/8 teaspoon salt
1/8 teaspoon cayenne pepper
1/8 teaspoon nutmeg

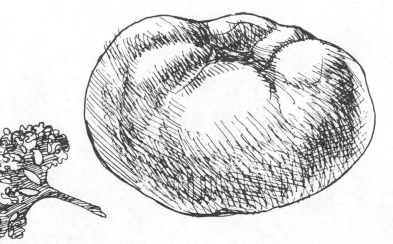

Spread the tomato slices over the bottom of the pastry shell. Sprinkle with onion and basil. Cover with the anchovies. Lightly beat the eggs with a wire whisk. Add the half-and-half and seasonings and blend until smooth. Place the pastry shell on a cookie sheet and carefully pour in the custard mixture. Preheat oven to 350°. Bake on the center shelf of the oven for 40 to 45 minutes, or until the top is puffed up and browned and a knife inserted in the center of the custard comes out clean. Remove from the oven and carefully slide onto a wire rack for 5 to 10 minutes to let the custard set. Garnish and serve hot.

ANCHOVY AND GREEK OLIVE QUICHE

1 pastry shell
2 ounces anchovy fillets, drained
1/2 cup sliced or chopped Greek olives
1/4 pound Feta cheese
5 eggs
2 cups half-and-half
1/8 teaspoon black pepper
1/4 teaspoon nutmeg

GARNISH
1 tablespoon finely chopped parsley
1 large Greek olive
Sprinkling of paprika

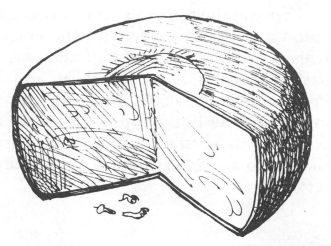

Arrange the anchovies in the pastry shell and spread the olives over them. Tear the Feta cheese and layer over the olives. Lightly beat the eggs with a wire whisk. Add the half-and-half and seasonings and blend until smooth. Set the pastry shell on a cookie sheet and carefully pour in the custard mixture. Preheat oven to 400°. Bake on the center shelf of the oven for 10 minutes. Reduce heat to 325° and bake for 30 minutes, or until the top is puffed up and browned and a knife inserted in the center of the custard comes out clean. Remove from the oven and carefully slide onto a wire rack for 5 to 10 minutes to let the custard set. Garnish and serve hot.

TUNA AU GRATIN QUICHE

1 pastry shell
7-3/4 ounce can tuna, drained and
    flaked
6 ounces Swiss cheese, grated
1/2 cup finely chopped onion
3 eggs
1-1/2 cups heavy cream
1 tablespoon lemon juice
1 teaspoon chopped chives
3/4 teaspoon garlic salt
1/2 teaspoon salt
1/8 teaspoon white pepper

GARNISH
Several parsley sprigs
3 lemon slices, cut in half
2 pitted ripe olives, thinly sliced
Sprinkling of paprika

146

Sprinkle the tuna over the pastry shell and add the grated cheese and onion. Lightly beat the eggs with a wire whisk. Add the cream, lemon juice, chives, and seasonings and blend until smooth. Set the pastry shell on a cookie sheet and carefully pour in the custard mixture. Preheat oven to 425°. Bake on the center shelf of the oven for 15 minutes. Reduce the heat to 350° and continue baking 10 to 15 minutes, or until the top is puffed up and browned and a knife inserted in the center of the custard comes out clean. Remove from the oven and carefully slide onto a wire rack for 5 to 10 minutes to let the custard set. Garnish and serve hot.

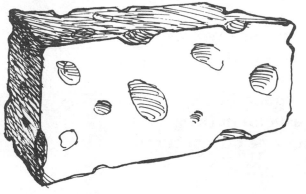

TUNA AND OLIVE QUICHE

1 pastry shell
7-3/4 ounce can tuna,
  drained and flaked
1 tablespoon grated onion
1/2 teaspoon Worcestershire sauce
2 tablespoons tomato paste
1 teaspoon lemon juice
1/4 teaspoon salt
1/8 teaspoon black pepper
4 eggs
1-1/2 cups heavy cream
1/4 cup dry white wine
1/8 teaspoon salt
1/8 teaspoon black pepper
1/8 teaspoon nutmeg
1/2 cup ripe olives, sliced

Put the tuna in a bowl. Mix in the onion, Worcestershire sauce, tomato paste, lemon juice, salt, and pepper. Spread the tuna mixture in the bottom of the pastry shell. Lightly beat the eggs with a wire whisk. Add the cream, white wine, and seasonings and blend until smooth. Set the pastry shell on a cookie sheet and carefully pour in the custard mixture, sprinkling in the olives at the same time. Preheat oven to 375°. Bake on the center shelf of the oven for 40 to 45 minutes, or until the top is puffed up and browned and a knife inserted in the center of the custard comes out clean. Remove from the oven and carefully slide onto a wire rack for 5 to 10 minutes to let the custard set. Garnish and serve hot.

TUNA AND SARDINE QUICHE

1 pastry shell
4-1/2 ounce can artichoke hearts,
  drained
2 whole pimentos, thinly sliced
6 pitted ripe olives, thinly sliced
7-3/4 ounce can tuna,
  drained and flaked
3-3/4 ounce can sardines,
  drained and flaked
4 eggs
1-1/2 cups half-and-half
1/2 cup chopped green onions
2 tablespoons chopped celery
3/4 teaspoon salt
1/8 teaspoon white pepper

GARNISH
4 stuffed green olives, thinly sliced
Several parsley sprigs
Sprinkling of nutmeg and paprika

Spread the artichoke hearts over the bottom of the pastry shell. Cover with the sliced pimentos and olives. Add the tuna and sardines and sprinkle with capers. Lightly beat the eggs with a wire whisk. Add the half-and-half, green onions, celery and seasonings and blend until smooth. Set the pastry shell on a cookie sheet and carefully pour in the custard mixture. Preheat oven to 375°. Bake on the center shelf of the oven for 45 minutes, or until the top is puffed up and browned and a knife inserted in the center of the custard comes out clean. Remove from the oven and carefully slide onto a wire rack for 5 to 10 minutes to let the custard set. Garnish and serve hot.

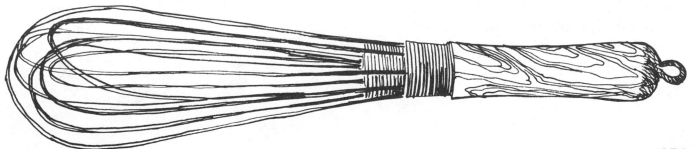

SALMON SOUFFLE QUICHE

1 pastry shell
7-3/4 ounce can salmon, drained
1 cup small curd cottage cheese
3 eggs, separated
1/2 cup heavy cream
1/2 teaspoon salt
1/8 teaspoon black pepper
1 tablespoon chopped chives
1 teaspoon lemon juice

GARNISH
2 pitted ripe olives, thinly sliced
2 stuffed green olives, thinly sliced
Several parsley sprigs
Sprinkling of paprika

Put the salmon into a large mixing bowl and beat with a heavy wire whisk until smooth. Slowly beat in the cottage cheese, egg yolks, cream, salt, pepper, chives, and lemon juice. Blend until smooth. In a separate bowl, beat the egg whites until stiff and fold into the salmon mixture. Set the pastry shell on a cookie sheet and carefully pour in the salmon-custard mixture. Preheat oven to 400°. Bake on the center shelf of the oven for 35 to 40 minutes, or until the top is puffed up and browned and a knife inserted in the center of the custard comes out clean. Remove from the oven and carefully slide onto a wire rack for 5 to 10 minutes to let the custard set. Garnish and serve hot.

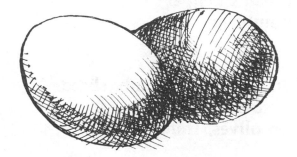

SMOKED SALMON QUICHE

1 pastry shell
1/4 cup chopped green onions
1/4 pound fresh smoked salmon,
    thinly sliced
1/4 pound Gruyere cheese, grated
4 eggs
1-1/2 cup heavy cream
1/4 cup dry white wine
1/8 teaspoon salt
1/8 teaspoon black pepper
1/8 teaspoon nutmeg

GARNISH
1/2 cucumber, peeled and thinly sliced
4 tablespoons sour cream
2 stuffed green olives, thinly sliced

Sprinkle the green onions into the shell and arrange the salmon on top. Sprinkle with the grated cheese. Lightly beat the eggs with a wire whisk. Add the cream, wine, and seasonings and blend until smooth. Set the pastry shell on a cookie sheet and carefully pour in the custard mixture. Preheat oven to 400°. Bake on the center shelf of the oven for 35 to 40 minutes, or until the top is puffed up and browned and a knife inserted in the center of the custard comes out clean. Remove from the oven and carefully slide onto a wire rack for 5 to 10 minutes to let the custard set. Garnish and serve hot. Garnish by dipping the cucumber slices in sour cream and arranging them over the top of the quiche, then adding the sliced olives.

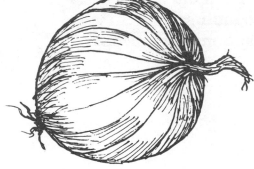

SALMON AND ENDIVE QUICHE

1 pastry shell
1 tablespoon butter
1 endive, shredded
1/4 cup beef stock (using 1 whole
   bouillon cube)
1 pound can salmon, drained and flaked
3 eggs
2 egg yolks
1 cup heavy cream, scalded
Rind of 1 lemon
1/8 teaspoon salt
1/8 teaspoon black pepper

GARNISH
1 cucumber, small, sliced thin
Several thin lemon slices, seeded
1/2 teaspoon dill seed
Sprinkling of paprika

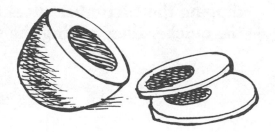

156

Melt the butter in a heavy skillet and saute the endive for a few seconds. Pour in the bouillon, cover, and allow to simmer for 30 minutes, or until most of the moisture has evaporated. Allow to cool slightly and spread the bottom of the pastry shell with the endive mixture. Spread the salmon over the endive. Lightly beat the eggs and the egg yolks with a wire whisk. Add the scalded milk, lemon rind, and seasonings and blend until smooth. Set the pastry shell on a cookie sheet and carefully pour in the custard mixture. Preheat oven to 350°. Bake on the center shelf of the oven for 30 minutes, or until the top is puffed up and browned and a knife inserted into the center of the custard comes out clean. Remove from the oven and carefully slide onto a wire rack for 5 to 10 minutes to let the custard set. Garnish and serve hot.

SHRIMP QUICHE

1 pastry shell
2 tablespoon butter
6 ounces shrimp, cooked and shelled
1/4 teaspoon salt
1/8 teaspoon black pepper
1/2 teaspoon tarragon
1/4 cup dry white wine
4 eggs
1-1/2 cups heavy cream
2 ounces Swiss cheese, grated

GARNISH
1 hardboiled egg, grated
Sprinkling of paprika

In a heavy skillet, melt the butter, add the shrimp, and toss gently for 2 minutes. Season with salt, pepper, and tarragon. Pour in the wine and boil rapidly until most of the liquid has evaporated. Spread the shrimp over the bottom of the pastry shell. Lightly beat the eggs with a wire whisk. Add the cream and blend until smooth. Set the pastry shell on a cookie sheet and carefully pour in the custard mixture. Sprinkle with grated cheese. Preheat oven to 375°. Bake on the center shelf of the oven for 30 minutes, or until the top is puffed up and browned and a knife inserted in the center of the custard comes out clean. Remove from the oven and carefully slide onto a wire rack for 5 to 10 minutes to let the custard set. Garnish and serve hot.

DANISH SHRIMP QUICHE

1 pastry shell
6 ounces cooked tiny shrimp
6 ounces Swiss cheese, grated
1/2 cup finely chopped onion
3 eggs
1-1/2 cups heavy cream
1 tablespoon lemon juice
1 teaspoon finely chopped chives
3/4 teaspoon garlic salt
1/4 teaspoon salt
1/8 teaspoon black pepper

Spread shrimp over the bottom of the pastry shell. Sprinkle with the grated cheese and chopped onion. Lightly beat the eggs with a wire whisk. Add the cream, lemon juice, chives, and seasonings and blend until smooth. Set the pastry shell on a cookie sheet and carefully pour in the custard mixture. Preheat oven to 425°. Bake on the center shelf of the oven for 15 minutes. Reduce the heat to 350° and bake 10 to 15 minutes longer, or until the top is puffed up and browned and a knife inserted in the center of the custard comes out clean. Remove from the oven and carefully slide onto a wire rack for 5 to 10 minutes to let the custard set. Garnish, if desired, and serve hot.

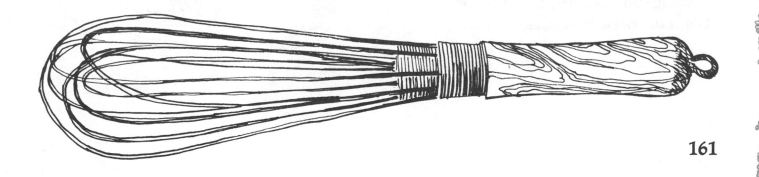

SHRIMP AND EGG QUICHE

1 pastry shell
3 tablespoons butter
3 tablespoons flour
1 teaspoon curry powder
1/2 teaspoon salt
1/8 teaspoon white pepper
1 cup half-and-half
1/2 cup dry white wine
9 ounces shrimp, cooked
6 hardboiled eggs, sliced
2 tablespoons chopped parsley
1/4 cup breadcrumbs

GARNISH
6 slices seedless lemon
Several parsley sprigs
    plus 1 tablespoon chopped parsley
Sprinkling of paprika and nutmeg

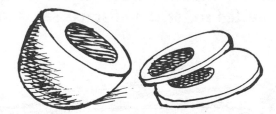

In a heavy skillet, melt the butter and add flour, curry powder, salt, and pepper and stir with a wooden spoon until smooth. Gradually add the half-and-half and wine and cook until thickened, stirring constantly. Stir in the shrimp, eggs, and parsley. Set the pastry shell on a cookie sheet and carefully pour in the filling mixture. Sprinkle with bread crumbs. Preheat oven to 350°. Bake on the center shelf of the oven for 20 minutes, or until the top is puffed up and browned and a knife inserted in the center of the custard comes out clean. Remove from the oven and carefully slide onto a wire rack for 5 to 10 minutes to let the custard set. Garnish and serve hot.

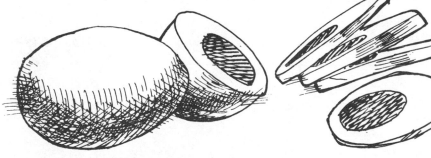

SHRIMP AND BROCCOLI QUICHE ORIENTALE

1 pastry shell
2 ounces fresh ginger
2 teaspoons cornstarch
1/4 pound shrimp, shelled and deveined
1 pound fresh broccoli
3 tablespoons vegetable oil
3 tablespoons sake or dry sherry
1 teaspoon salt
1 teaspoon sugar
3 eggs
1 cup half-and-half

Squeeze juice from the ginger with a garlic press. Combine juice with cornstarch, add shrimp, and stir to coat. Set aside. Split the broccoli into small pieces and steam or boil for 5 minutes, or until tender. Drain and set aside. Heat the oil in a heavy skillet and saute the shrimp, stirring constantly, until they turn pink. Add the broccoli, sake or sherry, salt, and sugar. Continue cooking until all ingredients are blended and coated with oil. Drain and spread over the bottom of the pastry shell. Lightly beat the eggs. Add the half-and-half and blend until smooth. Set the pastry shell on a cookie sheet and carefully pour in the custard mixture. Preheat oven to 350°. Bake on the center shelf of the oven for 30 minutes, or until the top is puffed up and browned and a knife inserted in the center of the custard comes out clean. Remove from the oven and carefully slide onto a wire rack for 5 to 10 minutes to let the custard set. Garnish, if desired, and serve hot.

QUICHE ROCKEFELLER

1 pastry shell
10 ounce package frozen chopped
    spinach
4 tablespoons sour cream
1 teaspoon horseradish
3-3/4 ounce can smoked oysters, drained
2 ounces Swiss cheese, grated
3 tablespoons grated Parmesan cheese
4 eggs
3/4 cup heavy cream
3/4 cup milk
1/2 teaspoon salt
1/8 teaspoon nutmeg

Cook the spinach according to package directions. Drain and dry thoroughly, pressing into a sieve to remove excess moisture. Place the spinach in a bowl and stir in the sour cream and horseradish. Spread the spinach mixture over the bottom of the pastry shell. Arrange the oysters on top. Sprinkle with grated cheeses. Lightly beat the eggs with a wire whisk. Add the cream, milk, and seasonings and blend until smooth. Set the pastry shell on a cookie sheet and carefully pour in the custard mixture. Preheat oven to 375°. Bake on the center shelf of the oven for 40 minutes, or until the top is puffed up and browned and a knife inserted in the center of the custard comes out clean. Remove from the oven and carefully slide onto a wire rack for 5 to 10 minutes to let the custard set. Garnish and serve hot.

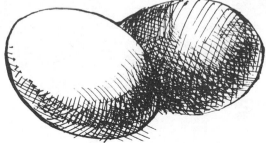

ANGELS ON HORSEBACK QUICHE

1 pastry shell
1/2 pound bacon
1/2 pound canned smoked oysters,
   drained
1/2 pound sharp Cheddar cheese, cubed
1/2 cup half-and-half
1/4 cup dark beer
1/8 teaspoon salt
1/8 teaspoon black pepper
1/4 teaspoon cayenne pepper
3 eggs

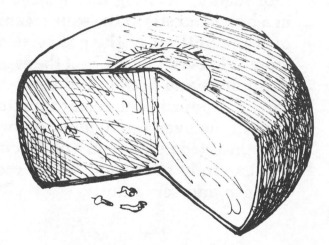

GARNISH
Several parsley sprigs
1 pitted ripe olive, thinly sliced
Sprinkling of nutmeg

Cut the bacon into small pieces and fry in a heavy skillet until crisp. Remove and drain on paper towels and set aside. Spread the oysters over the bottom of the pastry shell. Sprinkle the bacon over the oysters. In a small, heavy saucepan, melt the cheese over a medium heat. Blend in the half-and-half, beer, and seasonings. Lightly beat the eggs with a wire whisk and blend into cheese mixture. Set the pastry shell on a cookie sheet and carefully pour in the filling mixture. Preheat oven to 350°. Bake on the center shelf of the oven for 25 to 30 minutes, or until the top is puffed up and browned and a knife inserted in the center of the custard comes out clean. Remove from the oven and carefully slide onto a wire rack for 5 to 10 minutes to let the custard set. Garnish and serve hot.

SCALLOPS QUICHE

1 pastry shell
3/4 pound scallops
2 tablespoons finely chopped parsley
1/4 cup sherry
2 tablespoons butter
1/4 cup finely chopped onion
1/4 cup finely chopped celery
4 eggs
3/4 cup milk
1 cup heavy cream
1/4 teaspoon salt
1/4 teaspoon black pepper
1/4 teaspoon nutmeg

GARNISH
6 thin slices lemon
Several parsley sprigs
Sprinkling of paprika

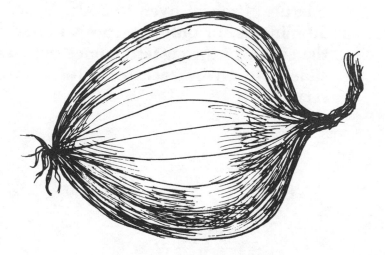

Combine the scallops, parsley, and sherry in a small bowl. Refrigerate for one hour. In a heavy skillet, heat the butter and add the onions and celery. Cook for 5 to 10 minutes, or until the onion is tender and golden. Lightly beat the eggs with a wire whisk. Add the milk, cream, and seasonings and blend until smooth. Add the scallop mixture and blend well. Set the pastry shell on a cookie sheet and carefully pour in the scallop-custard mixture. Preheat oven to 350°. Bake on the center shelf of the oven for 35 minutes, or until the top is puffed up and browned and a knife inserted in the center of the custard comes out clean. Remove from the oven and carefully slide onto a wire rack for 5 to 10 minutes to let the custard set. Garnish and serve hot.

MUSSEL QUICHE

1 pastry shell
2-1/2 pounds fresh mussels in shells,
   cleaned and cooked, or
   a 6 ounce can shelled mussels
4 eggs
2 egg yolks
2 cups heavy cream
1/2 teaspoon salt
1/4 teaspoon black pepper
1/2 teaspoon nutmeg

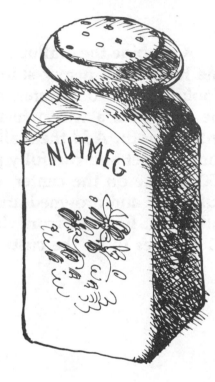

Spread the mussels over the bottom of the pastry shell. Lightly beat the eggs and yolks with a wire whisk. Add the cream and the seasonings and blend until smooth. Set the pastry shell on a cookie sheet and carefully pour in the custard mixture. Preheat oven to 350°. Bake on the center shelf of the oven for 30 to 35 minutes, or until the top is puffed up and browned and a knife inserted in the center of the custard comes out clean. Remove from the oven and carefully slide onto a wire rack for 5 to 10 minutes to let the custard set. Garnish and serve hot.

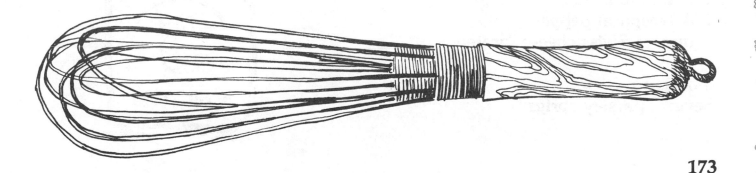

CRAB QUICHE

1 pastry shell
4 tablespoons butter
1/4 cup sliced green onions
1 cup fresh crabmeat
1/4 cup dry sherry
1/8 teaspoon salt
1/8 teaspoon black pepper
4 eggs
1-1/2 cups heavy cream
1/8 teaspoon salt
1/8 teaspoon pepper
2 ounces Swiss cheese, grated

GARNISH
Several parsley sprigs

Melt the butter in a heavy skillet and saute the onions until tender. Add the crabmeat, sherry, and seasonings and heat for just a minute. Set aside to cool. Lightly beat the eggs with a wire whisk. Add the cream and seasonings and blend until smooth. Combine with the crab mixture. Set the pastry shell on a cookie sheet and carefully pour in the crab-custard mixture. Sprinkle the surface with the grated cheese. Preheat oven to 375°. Bake on the center shelf of the oven for 25 to 30 minutes, or until the top is puffed up and browned and a knife inserted into the center of the custard comes out clean. Remove from the oven and carefully slide onto a wire rack for 5 to 10 minutes to let the custard set. Garnish and serve hot.

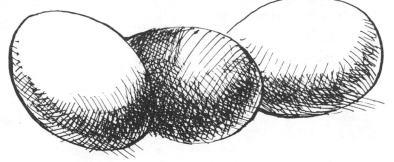

CRABMEAT AND AVOCADO QUICHE

1 pastry shell
1 large ripe avocado
2 teaspoons lemon juice
1/4 teaspoon salt
6-1/2 ounce can crabmeat, drained, or
   1 package frozen crabmeat, or
   fresh crabmeat
Dash Tabasco sauce
4 eggs
1-1/2 cups heavy cream
1/4 cup dry white wine
1/8 teaspoon salt
1/8 teaspoon black pepper
1/8 teaspoon nutmeg

GARNISH
3 pitted ripe olives, thinly sliced
3 anchovies, thinly sliced
Several parsley sprigs

Peel the avocado, cut into thin slices, and spread over the bottom of the pastry shell. Sprinkle with lemon juice and salt. To the crabmeat, add Tabasco sauce, and arrange in the shell. Lightly beat the eggs with a wire whisk. Add the cream, wine and seasonings and blend until smooth. Set the pastry shell on a cookie sheet and carefully pour in the custard mixture. Preheat oven to 375°. Bake on the center shelf of the oven 40 to 45 minutes, or until the top is puffed up and browned and a knife inserted in the center of the custard comes out clean. Remove from the oven and carefully slide onto a wire rack for 5 to 10 minutes to let the custard set. Garnish and serve hot.

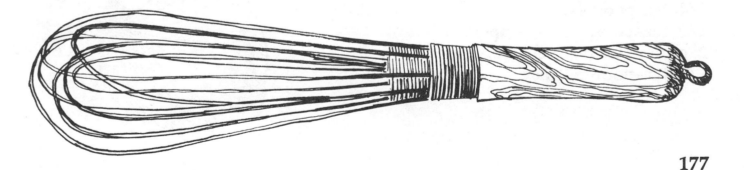

KING CRAB QUICHE

1 pastry shell
1 cup cooked Alaska king crabmeat,
  shredded
2 tablespoons mayonnaise
1/3 cup water chestnuts, chopped
1 tablespoon chopped onion
1/3 cup sherry
1 hardboiled egg, coarsely chopped
4 eggs
1-1/2 cups half-and-half
1/4 teaspoon salt
1/2 teaspoon white pepper
2 ounces Gruyere cheese, grated
1/2 teaspoon nutmeg

GARNISH
Several sprigs of parsley
1 hardboiled egg
Sprinkling of paprika

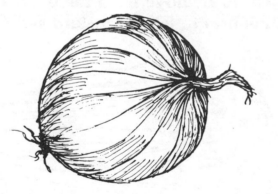

178

Place the crabmeat in a bowl and stir in the mayonnaise, water chestnuts, and onion. Add the sherry and blend until smooth. Add the chopped egg and stir into the crabmeat mixture. Lightly beat the eggs with a wire whisk. Add the half-and-half and seasonings and blend until smooth. Set the pastry shell on a cookie sheet and carefully pour in the custard mixture. Sprinkle with the grated cheese and nutmeg. Preheat oven to 350°. Bake on the center shelf of the oven 30 to 35 minutes, or until the top is puffed up and browned and a knife inserted in the center of the custard comes out clean. Remove from the oven and carefully slide onto a wire rack for 5 to 10 minutes to let the custard set. Garnish and serve hot.

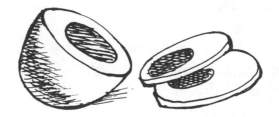

LOBSTER QUICHE

1 pastry shell
3 whole eggs
2 egg yolks
1 teaspoon Dijon mustard
1 teaspoon dry mustard
1 teaspoon salt
1 garlic clove, finely chopped
1/8 teaspoon cayenne pepper
2 ounces Gruyere cheese, grated
1/3 cup plus 2 tablespoons grated
    Parmesan cheese
8 tablespoons sweet butter,
    melted and cooled
2-1/2 cups half-and-half, scalded
1-1/2 cups cooked fresh lobster,
    shredded or flaked
2 tablespoons breadcrumbs

GARNISH
1 tablespoon grated Parmesan cheese
4 to 6 thin slices of lemon
6 whole shrimp, cooked and deveined
Several parsley sprigs,
    plus 1 tablespoon chopped parsley
Sprinkling of paprika and black pepper
1 pitted ripe olive, thinly sliced

Lightly beat the eggs and yolks with a wire whisk. Add both mustards, salt, garlic, and cayenne and blend until smooth. Mix in the grated Gruyere cheese, 1/3 cup of the Parmesan cheese, and butter. Pour in the half-and-half. Add the lobster meat. Mix with the whisk until thoroughly blended. Mix together the breadcrumbs and the remaining Parmesan cheese. Sprinkle over the pastry shell. Set the shell on a cookie sheet and carefully pour in the lobster-custard mixture. Preheat oven to 350°. Bake on the center shelf of the oven for 30 minutes, or until the top is puffed up and browned and a knife inserted in the center of the custard comes out clean. Remove from the oven and carefully slide onto a wire rack for 5 to 10 minutes to let the custard set. Garnish and serve hot.

LOBSTER QUICHE ROYALE

1 pastry shell
1 pound lobster meat, cooked
4 eggs
2 egg yolks
2 cups heavy cream
1/2 teaspoon salt
1/4 teaspoon black pepper
1/2 teaspoon nutmeg

GARNISH
Several parsley sprigs
1 pitted ripe olive, thinly sliced
Sprinkling of paprika

Cut the lobster into small pieces and spread over the bottom of the pastry shell. Lightly beat the eggs and yolks with a wire whisk. Add the cream and seasonings and blend until smooth. Set the pastry shell on a cookie sheet and carefully pour in the custard mixture. Preheat oven to 350°. Bake on the center shelf of the oven for 35 minutes, or until the top is puffed up and browned and a knife inserted in the center of the custard comes out clean. Remove from the oven and carefully slide onto a wire rack for 5 to 10 minutes to let the custard set. Garnish and serve hot.

EDIE'S QUICHE FRIDAY

1 pastry shell
4 eggs
1-1/2 cups half-and-half
1/4 teaspoon salt
1/8 teaspoon black pepper
1/2 teaspoon tarragon
1/2 pound crab meat, fresh or canned
1/4 pound shrimp, shelled, fresh or
    canned
10 ounce package frozen peas, thawed
2 ounces cheese, grated

GARNISH
Small tin sardines, well-drained
Several parsley sprigs
2 cherry tomatoes, thinly sliced

184

Lightly beat eggs with a wire whisk. Add the half-and-half and seasonings and blend until smooth. Slowly stir in crab meat, shrimp, and peas. Set the pastry shell on a cookie sheet and carefully pour in the seafood-custard mixture. Preheat oven to 350°. Bake on the center shelf for 35 minutes, or until top is puffed up and browned and a knife inserted in the center of the custard comes out clean. Remove from the oven and sprinkle grated cheese over top. Place under the broiler until cheese has melted and turned golden brown. Remove and set on a wire rack for 5 to 10 minutes to let custard set. Garnish and serve.

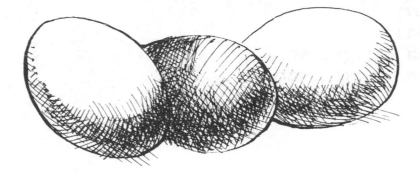

MIXED SEAFOOD QUICHE

1 pastry shell
1/4 pound halibut, cooked, flaked,
    and drained
1/4 pound lobster, cooked, flaked,
    and drained
1/4 pound shrimp, cooked, flaked,
    and drained
4 eggs
1-1/2 cups half-and-half
1/3 cup sherry
1/2 teaspoon salt
1/4 teaspoon black pepper
1/4 teaspoon summer savory

Mix the seafood together and spread over the bottom of the pastry shell. Lightly beat the eggs with a wire whisk. Add the half-and-half, sherry, and seasonings and blend until smooth. Set the pastry shell on a cookie sheet and carefully pour in the custard mixture. Preheat oven to 375°. Bake on the center shelf of the oven for 35 minutes, or until the top is puffed up and browned and a knife inserted in the center of the custard comes out clean. Remove from the oven and carefully slide onto a wire rack for 5 to 10 minutes to let the custard set. Garnish and serve hot.

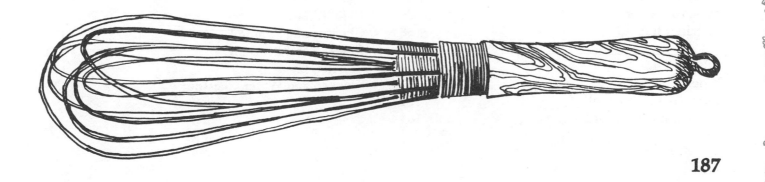

INDEX OF QUICHES

ANCHOVY
Anchovy and Green Olive 144
Anchovy and Tomato 142
Christmas 96
Spinach and Anchovy 92
Tomato 48

BACON
Alsace Lorraine 104
Angels on Horseback 168
Bacon and Mushroom 106
Bacon and Veal 108
Eggplant 56
Lorraine Henri 102
Mushroom and Bacon 80
Zucchini Bacon 68

BROCCOLI
Broccoli and Cheese 72
Chicken and Broccoli 134
Shrimp and Broccoli 164

CHEDDAR CHEESE
Angels on Horseback 168
Beef and Onion 126
Cheddar Links 122
Chile 94
Corn 76
Ham and Cheese 112
Onion and Cheddar 40
Tomato and Cheddar 50
Tomato/Cheese/Onion Ring 52
Zucchini Green Chile 68

CHILES
Chile 94
Zucchini Green Chile 68

CHICKEN
Chicken and Almond 132
Chicken and Broccoli 134
Chicken Liver 138
Chicken and Water Chestnut 136

COTTAGE CHEESE

Cottage Cheese	22
Salmon Souffle	152

CRAB

Crab	174
Crab and Avocado	176
Edie's Quiche Friday	184
King Crab	178

EGGPLANT

Eggplant	56
Moussaka	60
Ratatouille	58
Vegetarian	62

GREEN PEPPER

Cheddar Links	122
Christmas	96
Corn	76
Ham and Potato	114
Ratatouille	58
Sausage and Cheese	118
St. Tropez	98

GRUYERE CHEESE

King Crab	178
Leek	46
Lobster	180
Maison Edie	116
Smoked Salmon	156

HAM

Ham	110
Ham and Cheese	112
Ham and Potato	114
Maison Edie	116

LOBSTER

Lobster	180
Lobster Royale	182
Mixed Seafood	186

MEAT

Bacon and Veal	108
Beef and Onion	126
Curried	128
Lamb and Artichoke	130
Meat and Cheese	124
Moussaka	60

MONTEREY JACK CHEESE
Vermicelli 86
Zucchini Green Chile 68

MOZZARELLA CHEESE
Chile 94
Meat and Cheese 124
Mozzarella 24

MUSHROOM
Bacon and Mushroom 106
Chicken and Almond 132
Moussaka 58
Mushroom 78
Mushroom and Bacon 80

OLIVES
Anchovy and Greek Olive 154
Chile 94
Spinach Noodle/Mushroom 84
Tomato 48
Tuna and Olive 148

ONION
Alsace Lorraine 104
Cheddar Links 122
Chicken Liver 138
Corn 76
Crab 174
Curried 128
Danish Shrimp 160
Ham and Potato 114
Leek 46
Meat and Cheese 126
Moussaka 60
Onion 38
Onion and Cheddar 40
Onion and Swiss 42
Onion and Tomato 44
Ratatouille 58
Salmon and Endive 152
Sausage and Leek 118
Scallops 170
Smoked Salmon 156
Spinach 88
St. Tropez 98

Vegetarian Eggplant		62
Zucchini and Bacon		66
Zucchini Green Chile		68

OYSTERS

Angels on Horseback	168
Rockefeller	166

PARMESAN CHEESE

Ham and Potato	114
Italian Sausage and Cheese	120
Meat and Cheese	124
Mozzarella	24
Mushroom and Bacon	80
Onion and Tomato	44
Ratatouille	58
Rockefeller	166
Savory Potato	82
Spinach and Cheese	90
Tomato	48
Tomato and Vegetable	54

SALMON

Salmon and Endive	156
Salmon Souffle	152
Smoked Salmon	154

SAUSAGE

Cheddar Links	122
Italian Sausage and Cheese	120
Sausage and Leek	118

SHRIMP

Danish Shrimp	160
Edie's Quiche Friday	184
Mixed Seafood	186
Shrimp	158
Shrimp and Broccoli	164
Shrimp and Egg	162

SPINACH

Rockefeller	166
Spinach	88
Spinach and Anchovy	92
Spinach and Cheese	90

SWISS CHEESE

Broccoli and Cheese	72
Chicken and Broccoli	134
Christmas	96
Crab	174
Danish Shrimp	160
Eggplant	56
Ham	110
Ham and Cheese	112
Leek	46
Lorraine Henri	102
Mushroom	78
Mushroom and Bacon	80
Onion	38
Onion and Swiss	42
Onion and Tomato	44
Rockefeller	166
Shrimp	158
Spinach and Anchovy	92
Spinach and Cheese	90
Spinach Noodle/Mushroom	84
St. Tropez	98
Swiss Cheese	20
Tomato	48
Tomato/Cheese/Onion Ring	52
Tomato and Vegetable	54
Tuna au Gratin	146
Zucchini and Bacon	66

TOMATO

Anchovy and Tomato	42
Eggplant	56
Moussaka	60
Onion and Tomato	44
Spicy Cauliflower	74
St. Tropez	98
Tomato	48
Tomato and Cheddar	50
Tomato/Cheese/Onion Ring	52
Vegetarian Eggplant	62

TUNA

Tuna au Gratin	146
Tuna and Olive	148
Tuna and Sardine	150

ZUCCHINI

Ratatouille	58
Tomato and Vegetable	54
Zucchini	64
Zucchini and Bacon	66
Zucchini Green Chile	68